JESUS CHRIST

MASTER
OF THE
SPIRITUAL SCIENCE

Hadi F. Eid

Order this book online at www.trafford.com
or email orders@trafford.com

Most Trafford titles are also available at major online book retailers.

Book cover art "Against the Wind" courtesy of Artist Liz Lemon Swindle

Printed in the United States of America.

ISBN: 978-1-4669-7877-5 (sc)
ISBN: 978-1-4669-7876-8 (e)

Library of Congress Control Number: 2013904283

Trafford rev. 03/18/2013

Trafford
PUBLISHING   www.trafford.com

North America & international
toll-free: 1 888 232 4444 (USA & Canada)
phone: 250 383 6864 • fax: 812 355 4082

Contents

First Edition
January 01, 2013

"Greater is He that is in you, than he that is in the world. If you bring forth what is within you, what you bring forth will save you. If you do not bring forth what is within you, what you do not bring forth will destroy you."

Jesus

Prelude

By F. Paul Feghali PhD.*

"Blessed are they who hunger and thirst for righteousness for they shall be satisfied."

Jesus

The first Christian century while the Gospels were written, produced various currents promulgating knowledge and salvation. There were those philosophies emanating from the Hellenic world: the Epicurean that promotes ecstasy and prescribes its boundaries lest man wallows in pain; then the Stoicism depicting the world as a tiny village where man can control himself and his surrounding universe. There were also those mystifying beliefs flourishing in Egypt as well as in the Far East that stagger man into a maze of confusion where, even temporarily, his mind is estranged and emotions reign supreme outside the living world: an illusionary genus of Nirvana.

Many *teachers* emerged; some of them for a fee and others for the pleasure of priming disciples. Such was the delight of Justine in Nablus, Palestine who was gratified to see philosophy at last finding its way to Christ and is no more hanging theories without any stable foundations. Long was the time where a new philosophy discharges another leaving man torn and unfocused amid many orientations. We recall here St. Augustine who did not find salute until the day he heard that furtive voice in his garden: "behold, take and read!" What did he read? None else than the words of Christ; a *reading* that transformed the life of this forlorn lawyer that made his mother cry, into a great Christian teacher whose books are still read in our days especially his famous *Confessions,* where he chronicled his stumbling journey until he attained Christ.

Jesus Christ is the Master; thus he was repeatedly called by people. One of the Law scribes told him: "Master, I will follow you wherever you go" (Mat. 8:19). He called himself so when he sent away his disciples: "The disciple is not above his master." (Mat.10:24). And when the disciples felt the danger of drowning they screamed: "Master, you do not care that we perish?" (Mar.4:38). He also would warn believers who were bemused by the many Rabbis: "For *one* is your Master" (Mat.23:8). And when people dispersed after Jesus' hard talk and his asking the twelve whether they would walk away, Simon Peter answered him on their behalf: "Lord, to whom shall we go? You have the words of eternal life and we believe and are sure that you are the Christ, the Son of the living God." (Jo.6:68). Furthermore, Jesus described himself as such after washing the disciples' feet: "You call me Master and Lord; and you say well; for so I am." (Jo. 13:13).

Certainly Jesus is the Master; Master of the spiritual science indeed. Long the Gnostic movement claimed possession of the esoteric knowledge whereby no outside guidance is required be it divine or human. Such curtailed affinities were erroneously considered to restore salvation and redeem to the human being his lost harmony when he became alienated. Such conceptual process did not bring him back in or up to a higher level. The nature of the saved man is not bound to ethical ambiguities: he is like a pearl that remains a pearl even when trampled by dirt.

This conflicting acumen led to an outright inner human rift between two opposing principles. Man was in fact torn amid behavioral sloppiness and restrictive manners that prevent a philosopher for instance to eat meat, drink wine and practice sex. Thus we read Paul's epistles that confront such restraining, liberty suppressing tenets: "Touch not, taste not, handle not, which are all to perish with the using . . ." (Co.2:21.) While the real truth lies in Christ.

Paul discussed this *all-encompassing truth* that transcends consciousness to take hold of the total human: "In the past, when you did not know God, you did servility to those which by nature are no gods. But now, after that you have known God, or rather are known by God, how turn you again to the weak and beggarly elements?" (Ga.4:8). If you don't know God or you don't desire to know him, your idolatrous closing stages are similar to those you live within now; only knowing God elevates man and introduces him to His secrets through the Son, we are no more slaves but sons and daughters. "The servant knows not *what his lord does*."(Jo.15:15). Hence we are related because the Son *told us all he knows about the Father.*

Our conscious knowledge is fake and conducive to death while Jesus intended life for us and meant it in abundance. Erroneous knowledge drives man to servility, hence Jesus' insistence on "knowing the truth that would liberate you." John's Gospel highlights the special importance in *knowing* this truth that the Jewish elders starting with Nicodemus who came by night to Jesus, presumed they knew. Jesus showed him his ignorance as he pertains not to the celestial world but to the earthly one. Only if he is born again and moved from darkness to daylight the truth would be known to him. In his intense prayer before moving to passions Jesus declared: "This is life eternal that they might *know* You the only true God, and Jesus Christ whom You have sent." (Jo.17:3).

What kind of *knowledge* we are talking about? Scores of people *know* the Scripture and many have even memorized it; they hear but don't *listen,* they see but don't *observe.* They stop at the peripheries as Paul explained to the Corinthians: "Henceforth we know no man after the flesh, yes, though we have known Christ after the flesh, now we do not *know* him." (Co.5:16). This kind of knowledge seems meaningless. Crowds walked with Jesus and many pressed on him but derived no gains. When they implored him later: "We have eaten and drunk in your presence, and you have taught in our streets. But he shall say, I tell you, I know not from whence you are." (Lu.13:26). If God doesn't know them, how could they *know* Him?

Our real knowledge passion should befall in the spiritual, or better still the divine knowledge particularized further in this book. It ushers us into the mind of Christ which escorts and accompanies us through our pursuit to penetrate our human core and decontaminate it from all tares. Thus the latent subconscious in every human becomes enlightened consciousness with Jesus. He *knows* all of us and is in no need for reference on any man because "He knew all men and needed not that any should testify of man: for He *knew what was in man*." (Jo.2:24). Such is the real encounter conducive to *genuine knowledge*; otherwise we remain outside while the feast is in.

True knowledge consists of a sincere introspection coupled primarily with an insightful interpretation of the Scripture. This is the way to rediscover the true personality of Jesus who would greet us with a hug. Only then we dare say that the knowledge of the Father is truly within our grasp because "nobody knows the Father, save the son and he to whomsoever *the son will reveal Him*." (Ma.11:27). It is the Father's great pleasure to see us acquiring that *knowledge* that cements us with Him in an unconditional love.

Such is Hadi Eid's quest in his book "Jesus Christ, Master of the Spiritual Science." Following his first book "Jesus Christ that Unknown" that made waves among a vast American readership as well as the Arab world, he did not leave any thoughtless reader; in fact many have agreed, some disagreed and great many were doubtful. But isn't doubt a good entrance to faith? He, who does not reason and contend like Job, yields to conventional belief that imposes old postulates on his suppressed mind. That was not Hadi Eid's aspiration: he let fall all conformist, let alone traditional readings and adopted a process of psycho-spiritual interpretation ushering believers to new, unimaginable horizons. His work in the first book "Jesus Christ that Unknown" opened new avenues in religious thinking. He is pursuing an even deeper pattern in this second book taking our hands and minds into the mind of Christ, filling our hearts with his spiritual science.

These are new paths of spiritual thoughts we have navigated indeed. We leave it to others to tone with this poetic writer who heard the Master's words in the Scripture and took the helm not in passing the old but to give us an updated reading thereof commensurate with our accepted wisdom: "Every scribe which is instructed unto the kingdom of heaven is like unto a man that brings fourth out of his treasure *things new and old.*" (Ma.13:52). Hadi plunged and plunged and he incites us to plunge with him and discover the valuable pearl . . . Are we ready?*

---

*   Philosophy, theology & oriental languages. Sorbonne.

Foreword

"Look to the living one as long as you live, otherwise you might die and then try to see the living one, and you will be unable to see."

Jesus

Wen my previous book "Jesus Christ that Unknown" was published in the United States along with its Arabic copy in Lebanon, I received a lot of emails from various people either condemning or praising me for venturing into such an outlandish philosophy heretofore alien to the mainstream Christian belief.

Some wrote me saying: "What you say is not in the Scripture which is the word of God. So you cannot be correct," or: "The religious teaching I had received contradicts your ideas," or: "This is blasphemy that would take to purgatory or hellfire". A positive quote came from an eminent bishop: "I can't contradict you, but cannot promulgate your sayings"; and another reader stated: "I believe your book will be read 50 years from now!" The most moving plea however came, among others, from a devout villager relative of mine: "I can only tell you, I'll pray to God to save your soul!"

My answers were either thanks for just reading the book, or requests to read it again with a more open mind. As to my relative and his likes, I proposed to pray also to save their souls to come out even.

I had never blamed any of these people. I knew they wish to know and embrace the truth, but their subconscious mind has become so programmed with cumulative beliefs and insinuations constantly pushing them to beware whenever new questions of faith are at stake, especially when they believe they will be "punished" for such deviation. The old causes and effects of religion remain to them unapproachable taboos.

I never blamed them because "damned are those who sow seeds of doubt," said Jesus. My basic contention was that *peace of mind* is every human's sacred paradise; yet my constant consolation was again in Jesus' words: "I came not to send peace, but a sword." Such is the destiny for any contradicting theory. Those barely *satisfied souls*, required at a certain crossroad of their lives, some kind of a liftoff from the "milk food" they were grown up with, to the "adult food" as described by Apostle Paul, enabling them to rebuild superior wisdom, higher prudence and bolstered faith in this era of advanced knowledge.

Unlike the two other monotheist religions that can be described as learning/controlling systems teaching universal truths in understandable ways and *enforcing* their execution, Christianity came as a system of belief where the way is shown and people have the free choice to embrace and follow. This is the difference between the Law or Doctrine and the Grace conducive to the Truth. Hence, while Christianity seeks to enlighten and show the way, others seek to indoctrinate and control.

Jesus meant this enlightenment to be a free process. Belief should only emanate from personal conviction to become a pursuable way of life. A Christian is usually described a "born Christian"; he or she becomes officially so by the symbolic baptism initiated by John the Baptist which doesn't mean coming into the world with a Christian instruction manual. Hence Jesus' stressing on the later "born again" Christians or the spiritual adult renaissance as a prerequisite to enter the Kingdom of God. The fact that born Christians gain their religious habits at an early age from their parents, family and schools, implies that a further adulthood education is required to attain the true Christian competency.

Christianity is therefore a selective education, advocating what agrees with its objectives to elevate the individual to the divine status and not to control the masses. Freedom was not a mere slogan in Jesus' saying: "you know the truth, the truth will liberate you", but a far reaching advice to follow. The truth lies in his principles and instructions that he ushered men into their interpretation and assimilation with the God-given intelligence and free will; and not through churches, parents or relatives. Dealing with the mind of Jesus is a direct dialing and not through an operator.

Christianity today, especially its Catholic subdivision, is confronted with the theological problem of adapting its creeds and dogmas to a post-modern outlook and finding its place in a multi-cultural pluralist society. A New Thought approach is therefore due based on a *metaphysical* application of Jesus' teachings derived from the Gospels, to a world that is ripe for Universal Spirituality and steeped in a *scientific* way of thinking and explaining the universe. Jesus' mind and ministry must be re-interpreted for a new age.

To attain that important truth and be ready to enter the mind of Christ, you have to enter that "renaissance experience" or cleansing the subconscious mind by breaking the programming of your early years, retaining only what you believe within your inner being to be true, all the while remaining open to the expansive, joyful channels of the universe. The important truth begins to unravel that we are spiritual beings and aspects of the Universal, the Divine and Supreme Being: God. He inhabits our subconscious mind and wishes us the very best to fulfill our true destiny and evolve back to Him in perfection through experience. This is the essence of Jesus' teachings and such are the requisites of the Kingdom of God.

———◆———

In the beginning, God gave birth to his creation. But in the great mystery or wonder of the Virgin Birth, God became human and the Creator becomes the Created. This miracle is replayed and it happened to each one of us on a smaller scale when a human creates a work of art or intellect. In this same context, Gibran said about his masterpiece: "When I was writing The Prophet, The Prophet was writing me". This is also a far cry from what Jesus told his disciples: "When you speak, the Holy Spirit will speak for you". Whatever a human's mind conceives changes that same human as well because such conception is in a way his personal meditation or self examination. St. Thomas deliberated on this topic in his Gnostic "gospel" whereby in his passage 70, Jesus says: "If you bring fourth what is within you, what you bring fourth will save you."

The miracle in Jesus' birth is that he was not simply a recurring pattern of a human conception. Even when he was 12, Jesus did not repeat his parents' traditions and conflicts as humans do: "Did you not know I have to go about my Father's business?" He told his bewildered parents when they found him trading wisdom with the Temple's doctors. Jesus was born with that creative force that transcends the repetitive human cycle and breaks its chain of unconscious prototypes. This Creator/ Created paradigm alludes to the innate, most profound sense of co-creators we live and feel as a poignant impulse within us when we live in awareness. Great works however, may not be assessed for their values in their days, which is perfectly true for the chronicles of Jesus. He deplored the wasted exertions on miracles wrought in the cities of Galilee, although he knew that was his fundamental challenge to disseminate the *grain of wheat* philosophy.

Throughout this book, I have tried to dwell even deeper in the divine mind of the Master. Not to justify what I wrote in the previous one, but certainly to register nascent thoughts and rediscovered truths he tried hard to elucidate. Resorting to parables was perhaps his ultimate attempt to inject their meaning in the *deaf ears*—limited awareness—of his time. Hence his ultimate option to the eventful and final illustration: Death on the Cross. He recognized this dance between life and death as interplay between the temporal and the eternal, dark and light. In this divine performance he attained on the Cross the pinnacle of his life and showed us all the glorious results of sufferings and compassion.

Illiteracy was a problem in ancient times. The biggest obstacle Jesus faced was the lack of understanding among his listeners and even disciples. That obstacle persisted through early Christianity where people were told what to believe and because they could not research it for themselves they accepted the word from the only men they could trust: the clergy. The biggest problem today is that most people just don't find out religious information for themselves. The church doctrines have been passed down for generations and people, including the clergy, do not question them. This is a real travesty because there is a message within the message from Jesus but people only look at the literal interpretation. He spoke figuratively as was the trend in that era. He said "there would be a time I will tell you plainly about my Father."

Now we know why Jesus disseminated his philosophy through parables, again as grains of wheat, to germinate and bear fruits in this very era of advanced wisdom. He knew full well his disciples failed to grasp the underlying meanings of these parables as in the case of "The Sower", where he resorted to simplistic explanations suitable to their mental capabilities. Metaphors and exaggerations were therefore his way to indoctrinate hard conjectures into latent brainpowers. The Law of Attraction that was the mainstay in his teaching became only known to us in these days. Therefore when we read the Gospel, let us remind ourselves that it is not only a theological book, but rather one of encoded Metaphysics and Spiritual growth that could be understood by the free-thinking few. It is a book of initiation first and foremost.

Hence this new and updated reading; the gospels, to the extent they are original and impervious, support the Universal Truth through their metaphors, symbolism and parables. These have been greatly misinterpreted and misunderstood, let alone distorted. Need is therefore imminent to harvest the ultimate reality and display its known facts and meanings as straightforward as possible to mankind. Irrespective of their seeming objectivity, it remains necessary to penetrate their age old narration and garner the fundamental significance acceptable to our current thinking. We will be astonished to realize how befitting they are, as if they were disseminated for a much advanced era of sophistication: our own.

Unlike the people of the time of Jesus we can now find the answers for ourselves. We do not need an intermediary to tell us what and how to believe. If we want to get to the kingdom of God Jesus has already told us where and what it is. We have to be brave enough to analyze and question what we find instead of sticking our head in the proverbial sand. Jesus empowered us to get all the knowledge he had. Religion has been fear-based for centuries while the only way to know the truth is by free choice. That was the Master's intention in the first place. The information is out there and all we have to do is "seek the truth that will liberate us."

A case in point is what John said at the outset of his book: "In the beginning was the Logos, and the Logos was with God, and the Logos was God". The frequent mistranslation from the Hellenistic *"Logos"* into "Word" is theologically accepted while incorrect. "Logos" actually means "Thought," though it was used in the Hellenistic philosophy to denote "the Divine Mind that Controlled the World." In fact it is an important word with such profound meaning that surpasses the trite and simple connotation of "word". We will rename it "Thought Form", as it will appear repetitively further in this book when it becomes a vehicle for manifestation in the physical reality through the dimensional powers of the subconscious mind.

We will attempt to decode the true meaning beyond Jesus' parables and highlight the role of the human subconscious as indoctrinated by the Master, as well as the vibratory Law of Attraction initiated by him and rediscovered by psychiatrists two thousand years later. We will have a fresher look at Jesus who came to earth to teach the teachers, who would teach other teachers and all humankind how to live life happily and abundantly, and how to ascertain their very identity and realize their true destiny. The main purpose for this research is in no way religious but to shed new light on all inherited postulates that crowded people's subconscious due to chaotic upbringing, and also interpret the many valuable lessons for spiritual growth on this earth.

Before you indulge in further reading, a word to the wise: this is not a classical study, but a doctrine so powerful and freeing that it takes away any *baby food* religious upbringing you have acquired heretofore. This doctrine puts you in charge of your destiny the way Jesus intended and commended. It is like a subconscious fear of what might happen if people started believing they were their own masters. That would really create havoc in our current religious system, difficult for church people to accept. It is also a subliminal fear of responsibility and a realization that you are in control of your life and the master of your own destiny: a new and fearsome responsibility to accept because it means you can no longer blame circumstances, or fate or luck. It means that you are now *the sole reason for whatever is happening in your life.* Most people can't handle that. They would rather cling on to something else. They would rather blame it to something or someone else. Such are the negative recurrences clobbering every human, alien to the true Christian credo.

Return to Spirituality

*"Whoever drinks from my mouth will become
like me; I myself shall become that person, and
the hidden things will be revealed to him."*

Jesus

The two discernable characteristics of our age are on the
one hand a far-reaching interest in the deeper issues of
mind conducive to further spiritual realities, and, on
the other, a devastating and far-reaching materialism that is
apparent to all. We are witnessing these two life facets moving
along and side by side to say the least.

Yet we can perceive that spiritual life encompasses everything we do, and how we do it. All activities and circumstances are inherently "spiritual," and none stands in the way of spirituality. It is the way to find meaning, hope, comfort and inner peace in our earthly existence. Many people find it through religion, music, art or communion with nature. Others find it in their values and principles. Almost any human endeavor can be harnessed to spiritual progress and sustenance. True spiritual progress builds the ability to live appropriately and be happy, bright, and fulfilled under a larger range of opportunities.

Many believe that the spiritual motivation is taking over the materialist drive, and that we are witnessing another great step forward in this new episode of the human saga. There are many indications to this fact, chief among them is the feeling that materialism alone that attained its zenith is no more gratifying, and from the very constitution of the human mind and soul, it cannot support the searing urge to pursuit of happiness.

Spirituality is a matter of orientation. For a truly spiritual life, all we need is a constructive and responsible path to our obligations, good will and loving intentions toward our fellows, supported by faith in God and in ourselves. Spirituality may be also our apprehension, to a degree never equaled in human history, of the finer forces in nature, and using them effectively and usefully in the affairs and activities of daily life. It could be manifested as well in our realizing, understanding, and using the finer and higher insights of the powers of mind, spirit, and body.

Clear and noticeable laws of modern psychology have defined—and rather redefined many of the Master's teachings of "the Kingdom", given so far ahead in his time that people in general, and most of his disciples (all except Paul) in particular, were incapable of comprehending them. It is interesting and remarkable to realize that this new psychological finding, a new and vital content indeed in Christianity, has come about at this enlightened age; a surprising discovery that demonstrates in a concrete manner the fundamental principles of the Master.

Now we recall vividly how many times he felt the necessity of rebuking even his disciples for dragging his teachings down through their material interpretations. Some of the very esoteric truths he taught are now corroborated, fully understood and in some cases amplified by well-established laws of psychology causing mystery to recede into the background. The established fact nowadays is that speculation and conviction give way to a greater knowledge of the natural laws. The supernatural recedes as we dig deeper into the supernormal. The unusual loses its miraculous element as we gain knowledge of the law whereby things are being done. Now we realize that no miracle has ever been performed in the world's history that was not through the understanding and usage of laws. Jesus did prestigious miracles; because of his unusual knowledge of the rules through which they could be done. Otherwise, he would not induce our belief in the whole purpose of his teachings and injunctions. It was indeed the great longing of his heart when the people he came for, grasped the inner working of his mind.

Jesus' healing ministry was *scientific* because it utilized universal truths and principles, especially psychological and psychophysical ones. Hence he can be rightfully called the Master of the Spiritual Science and the pioneer in exploiting the hidden faculties of the human subconscious mind. His healing was not dogma-specific or limited to any religious tradition. In his spiritual teachings, the ministry of Jesus was for everyone and not to a chosen few in a specific religion. It was non-institutional and interfaith in scope. The *faith* required was simply that healing could occur, without favor or price, and such healing was, and is still now, available to anyone who recognized and realized Jesus' reality of wholeness and trusted his natural homeostatic process. Jesus, the Son of Man, was a spiritual scientist, and his methods are revealed through an analytical approach that follows the principles of Human Spiritual Mental Power (the Holy Spirit) nowadays expressed as the New Thought scientific approach. This study validates the insights of *metaphysical Christianity* that transcend any church religious specificity.

The relation between spirituality and physical conditions is a known fact. The body, mind and spirit, as we will see in details are interconnected. The well being of any one of these elements seems to affect the fitness of the others. Mental health and spirituality have a recognized connection that is being explored actively by psychotherapists and spiritual healers alike. Effective links have been established between psychology of the inner life and the transcendent practices of spirituality using joint technologies of Western psychology and Eastern spirituality; an exercise assumed earlier in history by Jesus himself during his 18 *lost years* among the Essenes* of Qumran. Many therapists recognize that the positive functioning of their clients is somehow improved by spiritual faith. They adopt mainstream religious experiences that connect meaningfully with modern-day psychology.

In this context, most therapists are reverting to analytical studies of the life and teachings of Jesus. In him, it is not difficult to trace the workings of a master healer and advanced psychotherapist. Though Jesus lived nearly 2000 years before Sigmund Freud and the giants of twentieth-century psychology, he demonstrated an understanding of the mind and emotions just as keenly as he understood the spirit of man. Jesus might indeed be called the founding father of psycho-spiritual healing. Many, through history (Deskalos of Cyprus to name one) who

---

* A Sufi-style Jewish religious group who believed among other things, in spiritual therapy and who secluded themselves in the caves of Qumran west of the Dead Sea and wrote the famous *scrolls*.

taught within a Christian context modeled their lives after Jesus and awakened among students and followers what it means to live a life of love.

Researchers have shown that matters such as positive thinking, comfort, strength and belief gained from meditation and prayer can contribute to healing and a sense of well-being. Improving your spiritual health may not cure an illness, but it may enhance your optimum feeling, prevent some health problems and help you cope with sickness, stress or death. Later on, we will gradually discuss how to enhance your spiritual health and identify the facts of life that bestow inner comfort and peace of mind.

Perhaps this peace of mind is the single, most important factor that drives people back to spirituality. People seek an accessible guide to live well in this fast, furious 21st century; a guide to surviving and thriving amidst the growing pressures of modern urban life and tuning in to the global spirit. This inner peace enables them to access a deeper spiritual self-understanding. Many have followed various popular prescriptions for enlightenment and still feel unsatisfied. They did not accost the fascinating guide of spirituality that will help them to grasp the great diversity of paths that are available to them. These are the time-tested tools of spiritual growth that usher in extraordinary depths of wisdom, power, and peace that motivated countless saints, mystics, masters, and sages since the beginning of history. Re-discovering your spiritual personality to realize boundless joy and a meaningful, lifelong journey is your God-given privilege.

Modern men and women do not have to go the mystic path to achieve true spirituality among the humdrums of daily life. Mysticism is just one of the love-driven ways of knowing God and feeling His presence in the inner self. It is no more exerting that effort of our mind to think through, capture, and describe the object of our belief in clear language, theological subtlety or scientific precision . . . a mystic is a person who has fallen in love with God, the quintessence of positivism, and has chosen his positive way that constitutes the shaping context and the compelling energy of our lives.

Christian mysticism is quite simply a contemplative spirituality. The word *mysticism* was intended to convey the sense that humanity cannot fully understand the *mystery* of God. Many fundamentalists used it to describe the paranormal or occult practices that *have never been* an element of Christian mysticism. Thus it became a contemplative spirituality, a way of focusing one's life completely on God through prayer, and living in love and awareness of His presence.

The more people of this century delve in its chaotic materialism, the more they crave the spiritual nourishment for their souls. They will grow even hungrier for the depth and meaning Jesus called *the full life* that he came to offer. His was a bountiful invitation to step in with both feet into a world of meaning and spirit. His 3-year ministry has taken mankind into many exciting and unusual adventures through every human's spiritual journey and inspirations that wake up the soul and keep it awake. An amazing journey charted by a heavenly Teacher!

Ever since the secular 1960s put forth their plucky challenge to the place of God in *a world come of age* spirituality has come back to life and kept rising and expanding like a yeasted lump of dough. Today, it is steadily asserting itself on ordinary saints in various parishes and has even ventured into academia. It may be hard to assess its facets in this religious climate but one salutary direction is evident: a return to the essentials of Jesus' teachings and extract major insights from their historical roots. Thus spirituality became an all-inclusive term to denote a way of life lived in response to the divine spirit. It balances an understanding with the might of God and the One who is in the midst of life dwelling with His bliss and blessing the very subconscious mind of every human. Thus spirituality drawn from Jesus' words is slowly orienting itself toward a future promise still to be realized prompting among other tendencies an essentially communal exercise to live love, obedience and service to our peers in humankind. A true implementation of the *Kingdom of God* directives and a modern style of *Christian discipleship* distinguished from doctrinal and systematic theology.

This nascent spirituality is gathering momentum by reconstructing a more natural and a more common-sense portrait of the Master. "It is the spirit that quickens," said he; "the flesh profits nothing; the words "Logos" that I speak unto you, they are spirit and they are life." Shall we recall again in this connection: "I am come that you might have life and that you might have it more abundantly?" When, therefore, we take him at his word and listen intently to his sayings and not so much to the words of others about him; when we place our emphasis upon the fundamental spiritual truths that he revealed in the simple, direct way, we are finding that the religion of Christ means a clearer and healthier understanding of life and its problems through a greater awareness of its elemental forces and laws.

Most clerics agree that spiritual maturity or spiritual fulfillment necessarily involves the *whole* person—body, mind, soul and relationships—in connection with the *whole* creation throughout the era of time. Spirituality encompasses the whole person in the totality of existence in the world, not some fragment or scrap or incident of a person. It is a lived experience and an effort to apply relevant elements in the deposit of Christian faith to guide men and women towards their personal progressive development which blossoms into ever increasing insight and joy. We all agree however that it has to do with our experiencing God and transforming our consciousness and lives as outcomes of that experience. It arises from a creative and dynamic synthesis of faith and life forged in the desire to live out the Christian faith authentically, responsibly, and fully.

Apostle Paul tells believers to be "filled" with the Holy Spirit. "Do not get drunk on wine, which leads to debauchery; instead, be filled with the Spirit." (Eph. 5:18). The flair in this passage is continual, and therefore means "being filled with the Spirit (Spiritual Mental Power)," or simply allowing the Holy Spirit to control us rather than yielding to the desires of our carnal nature. His apparently simple mentioning of wine carries in fact a deep insinuation: when someone is controlled by wine, he or she exhibits eerie characteristics such as slurred speech, unsteady walk, and impaired decision-making. Just as you can tell when a person is drunk because of the negative individuality he displays, so a born-again believer who is controlled by the Holy Spirit will display his positive characteristics. We find those in (Gal. 5:22), where they are called the "fruits of the Spirit." This is the Christian character, produced by the Spirit working in and through the born-again believer who exhibits a sound comportment and a consistent spiritual pace.

Paul's teachings embodied the perfect embodiment of Christian spirituality. He clearly distinguished between the "Spiritual Body" and the "Earthly Body". In his 1st epistle to the Corinthians he says: "There is a natural body, and there is a spiritual body. And so it is written. The first man Adam was made a living soul; the last Adam (Jesus) was made a *quickening spirit*. The spiritual was not first, but the earthly, and after that was the spiritual. The first man is of the earth, earthly; the second man is the Lord from heaven. As *is* the earthly, such are they also that are earthly, and as *is* the heavenly, such are they also who are heavenly. And as we have borne the image of the earthly, *we shall also bear (through renaissance) the image of the heavenly."*

This "renaissance", or being born-again, the cleansing of the subconscious mind in our modern interpretation, means that the believer receives the Holy Spirit, the spiritual mental power which Jesus promised it would lead us "into all truth" (John 16:13); the truth in taking the celestial characteristics and applying them to our lives where the Spirit is nowadays in control. Christian spirituality is based upon the extent to which a born-again believer allows the Spirit to lead and control his life, it is the decision we make to know and grow in daily relationship with the positive guidelines of the Master. When we breach those lines, we erect a barrier between ourselves and almost instantly feel we are soiling our born-again subconscious that emerged alert and alive. Thus, the Christian spirituality becomes a lived experience and discipline imprinting life with an oriented, self-transcending knowledge of freedom and love perceived and pursued in the mystery of Jesus. It becomes concerned with everything that constitutes the *Christian Experience* with its perception and pursuit of the highest interdisciplinary ideals that enriches the religious experience and promotes its development.

Much of the renaissance in contemporary spirituality has been given impetus by the Second Vatican Council. Its fundamental orientations underscored various contemporary understandings and denoted the importance of Scripture and its formative role in the spiritual life. Expressions of Christian spiritual life among the faithful cannot be measured, they relate to the specific context of how people live their relationships and the significance of culture that shapes these relations. This interpersonal and communal diversity prompted another current in contemporary spirituality with a perennial search for the true, authentic self. The reflection and reliance on interdisciplinary methods forge momentum from scriptural studies, developmental psychology, theology and history. Such approaches to the quest for true self are grounded in the conviction that human and spiritual developments are not opposing dynamics, but interrelated and complementary.

The return to spirituality evidenced by many Christians in this 21st century can be related to the advent of knowledge both of the human self and that of the environment. Ignorance enchains and enslaves and so, if not worse, is the half-culture. Truth, the clear and definite knowledge of the elemental yet esoteric laws of spirit, mind, and body, and of the universe about us conveys to freedom. This is delving into the spirit realm and exploring its inner, positive depths on the light of the newly elucidated Christian principles. Jesus exposed basically a spiritual philosophy of life. His whole revelation pertained to the essential divinity of the human spirit and the great gains that would follow the realization of this fact. The nascent knowledge enables humans to dwell into this spiritual reality anew, and harvest its many rewards. The Master's whole teaching revolved continually around his own expression, used again and again: the *Kingdom of God*, which he so distinctly asserted was an *inner state or consciousness or realization*; something not to be found outside the self but only within. Modern knowledge is allowing man to pervade that "within": the human subconscious mind. Yet this knowledge does not advocate a simplistic way to access this subconscious. It remains for many *the narrow door* Jesus pushed for and the epiphany that breaks through the mind and removes its worldly mask to become intimate with it. It is slaying the negative dragon while meditating upon it and dwelling with it for long days and hours much similar to Jesus' "temptations", suffering and enduring the pain of liberating our besieged mind. This is the shift in consciousness to access the subconscious where the "Logos (Divine Mind) is made flesh." This breakthrough is always preceded by some amount of frustration and suffering. In his book, The Prophet, Gibran writes: "Your pain is the breaking of the shell that encloses your understanding." Psychological suffering and sorrow often adorn the road to *heaven* in the Christian concept. No teacher or master can give that experience. It is something that must awaken in the individual. This leap forward, represents a shift in accessing the subconscious where all abstract issues come to life to become real and realized. Theology can function properly for humanity if unleashed to navigate in its proper context. The human spirit, long adhered to a theology that is several thousand years old, has now been raped by science. As a result, our religion has become impractical and impotent in today's world. Science and theology have drifted apart but science and mystical experience are quickly converging to reflect each other. The latest discoveries in science are very much aligned with the experience of the sage. The four Gospels, irrespective of their originality, still provide life, mystery and metaphors all applicable in today's world. They were born out of that authentic and creative spirituality.

Nietzsche once significantly proclaimed that God was dead, a well aligned thinking with many modernity trends. Modernity has been inaccurately equated with secularism, while religion more closely meshes with pluralism and becomes enriched with the seeds of spirituality. Some interesting facts can be gleaned from various world societies: China for example is set to become one of the most populous Christian countries with 100 million Christians, and five of the ten biggest megachurches in the world are not now in Europe, but in Korea. Jesus' spirituality is taking over Buddha's for two main reasons: one, because the first is interacting suitably with the advent of culture while Buddha's is still shrouded in seclusion, and two because Buddha is dead while Christ is alive.

Distinct evidence shows day after day that religious people are healthier, wealthier and wiser. What is interesting about science at the moment is the emergence of vocal scientists with ever more elaborate and rational reasons why God should exist. With the alien and worldly definitions of God outside Jesus' philosophy depicting Him as the Father residing in our inner self, Nietzsche could be right; but entering Jesus' mind to redefine God, his theory would cede grounds to the spirituality that looks once more in the right path.

Our Angels and Demons

"I will praise You, for I am fearfully and wonderfully made; Your works are marvelous and my soul knows it very well."

Psalms

This is how David praised God for His marvelous works within his wonderfully made human body. He could not fathom the inner energy that governs this body and produces those positive or negative feelings that "his soul knows very well." This amazement does not cease to hang around in us today enticing us to further wonderings. So what is the origin of this positive/negative phenomenon?

The human body is run by an intricate electric circuitry. This low-voltage power directs and regulates many bodily functions; chiefs among them are the heart, the brain and the subconscious mind. The body electricity is light in a sub-material state; it is made of streamlined positive and negative currents. Its importance to the inner life of the human being is in the greatest contrast and the constant mixture of good and evil. Electric power engulfs all human and animal surroundings. Our earth interior emits natural micro-pulsations at an approximate rate of 10 oscillations per second. Lightning creates fields in a frequency range of thousands of oscillations per second while the spectrum light is visible with billions of oscillations. Throughout the evolution of human consciousness, humans were closely united through physical bodies with this ambient world of matter in relation to thinking, feeling and willing.

The human energy field contains and reflects all individual's impulses. It carries the emotional dynamism created by the internal and external experiences both positive and negative. This emotional force influences the physical tissues within a human's body where the individual's biography or the cumulative life experiences become his biology. The emotions generated through these experiences develop into an encoded record in his subconscious mind, the central motor of all biological systems, and contribute to the formation of cell tissues which then generate a quality of energy that reflects those positive or negative emotions.

Medical science established today that our bodies have *sensory receptor cells* with different types of physical stimuli that are changed into electrical signals. Billions of neurons keep moving throughout our nervous systems carrying electrical pulses to and from our brain. Dr Werner Gitt, a pioneer in studying the body's electrical power says, "If it were possible to describe the nervous system as a circuit diagram with each neuron represented by a single pinhead, such a circuit diagram would require an area of several square kilometers . . . it would be several hundred times more complex than the entire global telephone network; it may be likened to a switch which is turned either on or off according to the right conditions. The impulse is not generated unless the neuron has been given a strong enough stimulus. It is hard to imagine the complex integration of electrical signals without realizing the Creator's power and wisdom."

Equally difficult is to understand how the nervous system, particularly the brain, could have been produced by evolutionary randomness and selection. We have barely touched on some of the electrical design present in the rest of the body. The truth is that scientists are always discovering more about its workings since its complexity surpasses by far anything produced by man and is nothing short of a miracle. Truly we can say with David, "Your works are marvelous and my soul knows it very well."

Many aspects in this existence don't make sense at first encounter. We feel them and live them without being able to justify them. One such aspect is the positive and negative energy affecting the minds of the human race that is usually related to angels and demons. That seemingly unknown, unseen energy affects the thoughts of men and women to either do good or bad in their life. The positive energy is that of angels, or our *angelic nature* and the negative energy the demon, our *devilish nature* . . . When we realize the existence of the two influences in our world we drop the veil of ignorance and see what the mind cannot comprehend at first, but in time one can learn to feel the presence of positive and negative energy in form of thoughts, impulses and behaviors.

Man's internal struggle between his positive/negative currents pushed him to identify them by a more blatant phenomenon: the angel and the devil. He erected mental as well as material temples to glorify or condemn them being the sources of either his bliss or misery. Today there is a growing awareness in feeling and discerning this dual energy, how we become immersed in its functioning and to what extent we can deliberately control any of the two currents to achieve mastery over our happiness or misery.

When we are entangled by our negative energy, our thoughts will lead us away from positive thinking to a mental state where we cannot think for ourselves freely. Our will power becomes paralyzed and our mind displays negative outlooks on life. This is the "demoniac" way to block out control and make us feel ashamed of ourselves driving our self-respect and self esteem to negative aspects and tearing down the self-image we had struggled all along to build and fortify. Jesus described this phenomenon when he said: "The thief (Satan, the negative prince) comes to steal and kills and destroys (all positive buildups), I have come that they might have life (positive beatitude), and have it to the full (entirely positive)" (John 10:10.) This negative functioning is easily identifiable the moment it takes place in your consciousness where you feel your "angelic side" gently warning you that an imminent attempt by your negative "demon" to take hold and consume any positive powers you had accumulated is looming near.

On the opposite and bright side, your "angelical," positive energy, makes you feel good about yourself. It reinforces your self-image and makes your inner light shine bright . . . the more you control the positive energy—by injecting positive thoughts and feelings, the brighter your light will shine in the core of your consciousness. The positive energy of angels works in the opposite way than the demons; they whisper their soft angelic voices in your subconscious mind pointing you to the right direction where your Thought Forms take their prescribed universal path toward manifestation. Slowly but surely, that soft voice in your consciousness becomes a lot stronger and that you are more able to make the right or positive decisions in your life when time comes to make them. This is what Jesus meant in saying: *"He who has will be given and added, and he who has not will be taken from."* Positive energy plays by the universal rules whilst negative demons have no rules but only a series of tricks in an attempt to break the ideals of your subconscious.

A human feels the positive energy as a *surge of personal power* within his body; while negative impulses as an obliteration to this power. In Christ's words this is a *"High or Low in Spirit."* Positive and negative experiences register a memory in cell tissues as well as in the energy field. Our emotions reside physically in our subconscious mind and interact with our cells and tissues because the same kinds of cells that manufacture and receive emotional chemistry in the brain are present throughout the body.

What gives the emotion its positive, neutral or negative energy however is how such emotion is portrayed and interpreted by each individual. Anger, for instance, "burns" like fire and, expelled outwardly in a rough manner, it accentuates its negativity; yet when harnessed it can be the igniting spark for a positive change. Love on the other hand, is like flowing water that saturates all that it touches and tender loving moments can be the most positive of feelings that enriches the human spirit. Love reigns atop all positive human feelings.

GOD
The Holy Spirit

Positive	*(HumanPower)*	Negative
ANGEL		DEVIL

Feelings:

Love	Hatred
Joy	Sadness
Belief	Doubt
Kindness	Badness
Compassion	Coldness
Enthusiasm	Apathy
Moderation	Cupidity
Praise (justified)	Criticism
Calm	Anger
Thoughtfulness	Cruelty
Purity	Impurity
Courage	Cowardice
Equanimity	Agitation
Decisiveness	Hesitation
Openness	Reticence
Attractiveness	Repulsiveness
Truthfulness	Dishonesty
Loyalty	Perfidy
Moderation	Greed
Altruism	Selfishness
Contentment	Envy
Wisdom	Foolishness
Etc . . .	Etc . . .

Peace of Mind	Struggle within

"Heaven"	*"Hell"*

Paul's Galatians epistle depicts clearly—even through elementary thinking—the human negative and positive paths: "the acts of the sinful nature are obvious: sexual immorality, impurity and debauchery; idolatry and witchcraft; hatred, discord, jealousy, fits of rage, selfish ambition, dissensions, factions and envy; drunkenness, orgies, and the like. I warn you, as I did before, that those who live like this will not inherit the Kingdom of God . . ."

Following the positive path is the best and quickest way to improve your life, even changing it. You have probably heard this many times before. And you're probably thinking, "That is a great idea, but in the real world it is easier said than done." It is true; like a lot of things in life, becoming a "positive" person is an idea that is *simple* but not necessarily *easy*.

Still according to Emerson, "Actions and feelings go together and we can control the feelings by controlling the actions." Anyone of us can set for himself, depending of his will power and capability; practical and available techniques to make positive thinking an automatic and permanent part of his/her life.

The first step is to convince oneself how critically important the positive thinking is. Our *thought patterns* have a huge influence over every aspect of our life. They are the vehicles carrying our aspirations to the subconscious mind where they are imprinted to become the imperative determinant of our personality. You can become a positive thinker by discarding, one by one, your habitual negative thought patterns. The first step brings us to the diagram above where we notice that "Joy" comes next to Love in the positive echelon. Laughter makes the soul and the body "happy." Apparently moving facial muscles sends signals to the autonomic nervous system which controls certain muscle and gland activity. This in turn spurs the physical reactions. Are you unable to smile or laugh due to many anxieties? Use Emerson's guidance and induce yourself to laugh. And when you do, you trigger your own mechanism toward a positive feeling that will continue to build up: *you are now a positive individual*!

The second step on the positive road is to choose your words carefully. The most dangerous words we hear are "can't." and "don't." How often you hear people saying: "I can't lose weight, or I can't stop smoking . . ." Their repetition becomes *reality*: a subconscious imprint. *Do not let these words steal your true potential.* More venomous than words is the negative talk you address to yourself: "I'll catch cold" or "I'll never make it." These are the seeds of doubt that limit your capabilities and invite troubles. And the worst of all is the faithless affirmation; Carl Jung says in this respect: "*What you resist persists.*" Shakespeare puts it in simpler words: "Our doubts are our traitors;" you should be aware of your negativities to be able to eject them. They appear at their best when you sit alone with your subconscious, and when you do, remember this: *You are what you are when you are alone.*

Being alone means you are in meditation, the ultimate introspection exercise you can ever attempt. This is where you train your brain to increase your positive thinking power and put your life priorities in their proper perspectives. This is the visualization process inherent to contemplative exercises and the funnel of positive energy that flows through the top of your head. This positive energy comes from the purist, highest, most divine source of energy in the universe that Jesus called Father. It is the Holy Spirit; and the moment it enters your body you sense its positive, loving, and healing effects. You feel it cleansing you gradually of negative tares; washing away any past harmful programming that affected your subconscious mind. Any time you need a lift, allow the visualization to take its course and feel revived and purged of any negativity.

"Fear not, only believe;" said Jesus to Peter. Fear and Faith are as opposing forces as the negative and positive in our spiritual power. The more we reinforce our positive potential the more we bolster our faith. No one goes through life without problems or obstacles. Life is a game to the believer who looks for an advantage or opportunity in any situation and a horrible test to the faithless who gives up at the first fall. The believer dwells on willpower while the faithless pictures a negative end result. Let me here repeat the old adage: "If you believe you can, or believe you cannot, you are right!"

The fertile human imagination went wild across centuries depicting its negative features through many *satanic* peculiarities. They were all hideous, repulsive and vile. Satan was painted in thousands of abhorrent forms. To the elders' superficial minds as well as to our children today, the devil has a trim, black body, with horns, malicious eyes, a long tail and carries a pitchfork. He lives in hell and loves to torture bad ignorant adults as, in our times, little children. Children are not born with these ridiculous beliefs; they learn them from mislead parents who in turn inspire them from the Church. Many use this fear of the devil to persuade children to behave. It is apparently very important to instill fear at an early age; this has unfortunately become a basis in our religion.

God may not end this world we know and enjoy. But negative energy will freeze life and its quality. God is not responsible for implanting the negative force for the purpose of empowering the human being with a whole energy. Only humans who pursue their negative thoughts, plans and actions are responsible. Negative breeds only negative causing a chain reaction of destructive events not because of some self imposed sentence by God, but because of the consequences of intense negative energy blindly emitted by the human race.

The Father

"Follow your bliss and the universe will open doors for you where there were only walls"

Joseph Campbell

W here is God and what are His features? This recurrent question haunted my imagination since my high school years. Even before that I was asking my teachers: "exactly *where* or *what* is the secret place of the Most High?" I could not accept He was in Heaven: if so, was He in the atmosphere, the troposphere, the space beyond or somewhere in the vast firmament? Is He on a throne surrounded by angels as the Western imagination depicts Him in countless paintings or is He in the Seventh Heaven or on a throne over the water as Islam narrates? Is He a Soul as in the Scripture? And is that Soul similar in shape to that of a Man?

Most of the time my teachers made up a nonspecific answer on the spot or gave me some spiritual cliché, but nobody was able to give me a straight answer. It was *so very important* for me to find this *secret place*, because I wanted to *dwell there*. Is God currently revealing where He is located? To my amazement, these and other questions were plainly answered by Jesus: the *secret place of the Most High* is not in Heaven or *in the Garden of Eden* but in our mind in as much as *the mind of Christ*! Jesus referred to God as "the Heavenly Father" and even taught us to pray "our Father who is in Heaven" only to bestow Him the due eminence and distinction innate in the human mind.

Neither the Old Testament, nor the Koran could accept a God who is so human. Their great protest is that it is not suitable to speak of God in this way, He must remain pure Majesty. Majesty full of mercy, certainly, but full of wrath as well. His mercy should not exceed the point of paying for the faults and sins of His own creatures. Since the dawn of humanity man coveted a Super being much above his stature to revere and worship. Other clerics and philosophers wrote volumes evolving around the big question: "If God exists why is He hiding?" But God revealed his secrets to His sons and we are His sons as much as Jesus is. We dwell with our minds and this is where God dwells. Our subconscious mind is the *only* realm of God, and this is where we can meet, *see* and interact with Him.

Jesus treated this subject time and again with full transparency and insisted on us to identify with it: *"Then answered Jesus and said unto them, Verily, verily, I say unto you, the Son can do nothing of himself, but what he sees the Father do: for what things soever He does, these also does the Son likewise. For the Father loves the Son* (interfaces with him), *and shows him all things that Himself does: and He will show him greater works than these, that you may marvel".* (John 5:19.)

What Jesus is saying here and metaphorically meaning all of us, is that he can do nothing in and of himself. Jesus, the physical person, has no inherent abilities by virtue of who he is, only God "does things" through him; in other words Jesus is a channel of experience and expression for God who loves His Son—because of his perpetual dwelling in Him—as he does all of His children, all of us who follow Jesus' steps; It is that plain and simple: those Unconditionally Loved Children of God can have *anything* through Him, irrespective of its type or magnitude.

Thomas as well as Philip, the skeptic minds having millions of equals in our era, insisted on Jesus for a palpable proof of the Father: "Show us the Father, asked Phillip, and it suffices us." Jesus told him: *"Believe you not that I am in the Father, and the Father in me? The words that I speak unto you I speak not of myself: but the Father that dwells in me, he doeth the works. Believe me that I am in the Father, and the Father in me: or else believe me for the very works' sake. Verily, verily, I say unto you, He that believes on me* (follow my path), *the works that I do shall he do also; and greater works than these shall he do;* (exactly as done later by Peter and John) *because I go unto my Father. And whatsoever you shall ask in my name, that will I do, that the Father may be glorified in the Son. If you shall ask any thing in my name, I will do it."* (John 14:10.)

Jesus could not be more explicit in his statement: It is "the Father that dwells within him that does the works." The important thing is his showing himself, as well as any fellow human, as an equal and inseparable aspect of God. He wants us to believe God is within us and realize He is the true source of our power. This is the veritable meaning of "Faith," when we believe that the God-given power is our existent reality and power, and when we implore the father we accept him as the *Source within*. Without this connection we cannot achieve anything. This is the powerful truth that unleashes our full potential and ability as children of God where our feats and achievements become "glorified."

Jesus rightfully allocated to God the all-encompassing name: "Father." For one, the old, trite term "god" was a recurrent designation of all kinds of deities. On the other hand, "father" implies that loving, caring and nurturing connection craved by all humans. Many modern names have been bestowed to God: The Source, the Universal Mind, the Divine Providence . . . Yet "Father" connotes that intimacy and relationship inborn in the human being toward his deity, that reliable, divine support that is close to them and not away in the firmament; the father-son relationship was the answer.

Jesus humanized God for yet another rationale that characterized the whole Christian creed: among the three monotheist religions he elevated man from a "slave of God" stature to the "son of God" distinction. The Mosaic Law, out of humble and deep submission to the Almighty, enslaved man to his creator and established the "slave-master" modus as the only permissible interaction. Islam later echoed the Hebraic belief and even went steps ahead in confirming man's servility to the overall mighty divinity. This servility, meant to imply humbleness among adherents of both religions, became false-modesty in real life applications.

Jesus opposed this approach and raised man to a higher pedestal: "I do not call you servants [or slaves] any longer," he told his own, chosen community. In an era where slavery can have many bad names that was indeed welcome news. The larger problem of slaves is that they are "en-slaved" to a blind obedience. They are not given the whole scope of things. They do not make decisions. They merely follow along in a kind of legal obedience to their master. Jesus reversed this cycle and taught that neither he nor the Father is that kind of master. In that new process where the one who is getting served was not served for the sake of the slaves' own skin, a community of love manifested itself: the absolute obedience was transformed into one of a deliberate, joyful covenant.

Jesus meant this partnership to become a fountain of life, watering the soil for an ever-greater human harvest that makes man a joint heir of God. It lights his way and lightens his burden enabling him to live in the consciousness that the Father works within him: "my Father works and I work." With this understanding a man finds out he is not alone; the more fully he realizes this the more he finds himself conscious of an enlarging reception of life, light, energy and power. Man is born in a consciousness surrounded by countless limitations. This knowledge of a higher consciousness, the consciousness of the spirit of God within him, dissipates slowly but surely such limitations. It is the feeling of being born anew from above. This new birth opens up and activates in anybody's life possibilities and powers that otherwise lie dormant and dead. It is the nature of the Father to give good gifts unto His children; and those who have faith will attain full realization in life and thereafter.

Jesus raised man to such partnership for yet another, heretofore totally uncovered reason: The heavenly Father dwelling in us does not sin. God designs and designates the positive path and wants humans to follow the same trail. A raised man to the deity's order is automatically reminded through the repeater of his subconscious mind to follow the same positive highway, heave himself from the negative aspects of human feebleness and chart a lifeline prescribed by the sublime impulses of his educated subliminal self. *This is the leap from slavery to partnership that entails higher responsibilities*, renewed dynamism and vigilant alertness. Perhaps for that reason Jesus, almost in all his speeches, called for such watchfulness to become aware and live up to the commands of the new conscientiousness. Commands that are far from the abiding relationship: a free will bind that has the blessing of the personal self prior to the heavenly one.

Here lies the powerful truth with which we can realize our full potential and abilities including the command to perform what we regard as "miracles." Jesus was the full personification of the Source of Power and repeatedly attributed to that Source all his miracles: "The Father within Him, He does the works." He stated that we shall do even greater things than him because we are unlimited, infinite and immortal aspects of "the Father." Paul puts it modestly in his epistle to the Corinthians: *"Now there are diversities of gifts, but the same Spirit. And there are differences of administrations, but the same Lord. And there are diversities of operations, but it is the same God which works all in all. But the manifestation of the Spirit is given to every man to profit withal. For to one is given by the Spirit the word of wisdom; to another the word of knowledge by the same Spirit; To another faith by the same Spirit; to another the gifts of healing by the same Spirit; To another the working of miracles; to another prophecy; to another discerning of spirits; to another divers kinds of tongues; to another the interpretation of tongues: But all these works as one and the selfsame Spirit, dividing to every man severally as he will. For as the body is one, and hath many members, and all the members of that one body, being many, are one body: so also is Christ.* (1Cor.12:4.)

A commanding message indeed asserting a fundamental issue: There is one Source who created everything that works through each and every one of us in various ways. This "one body" has "many members" each of which is a different but integral divine aspect. The creation, large or small as perceived by humans, constitutes the *many members* of God and the *many channels* that make up the whole experience through which God is *glorified*. We each have our place and no *member* is superior in any way to any other member despite human traits, power or control. Yet this depicts *our role within* the magic of this stature and entices us to live it every moment just as Jesus did; we then acquire not only the same powers as Jesus but even greater because God within us *does the works* and his powers are limitless.

Once we *feel* this Sublime Presence within our subconscious our wishes, needs and desires become a joyful experience to realize, our true reason for being here clarified and the answers to our various needs forthcoming: *"Ask, and it shall be given you; seek, and you shall find; knock, and it shall be opened unto you: For every one that asks receives; and he that seeks finds; and to him that knocks it shall be opened."* (Mat.7:7.)

This Sublime Presence is the Holy Spirit that Jesus advocated to make the Dwelling of God within us more conspicuous. The Spirit gives various *gifts to build ourselves up* and intercedes for us as it intercedes for the saints in accordance with God's will" (Rom. 8:26.) In modern terms this is not only received communication but broadcast as well. It implies intelligence, concern, and a formal role. Thus the Holy Spirit is not an impersonal or an outlandish power, but *an inherent and built-in intelligence that lives within us triggered by the divine helper.*

Again, the advent of science, predicted until recently as enemy of Faith and spirituality is putting Christian theology today in a credibility crisis; so long as theological squabbles in matters of nature and Earth/human relationships conflict with the human experience the credibility issue intensifies. We need to take seriously the radical truth of Pope John Paul II that heaven is not a "place in the clouds" but rather a *relationship with God.*" A deeper insight into the *scripture* of the universe informs respectful relationship; thus the case for replacing in religion its static-centrist worldview with the transformational process should be pursued. Until this quantum leap in theology is achieved the frustrating religious wavering will linger.

Jesus proved his divine authority by revealing these ways to his disciples and many audiences to the extent of extraordinary works that he wrought including suspensions of the laws of nature. They are illustrations of the power of mind over matter, of the spirit over the flesh. For the accomplishment of such miracles we have the express authority of Jesus himself. Although he ascribed his extraordinary work directly to God but also declared they were wrought by faith; basing his authority as the Son of God not upon any departure from the laws of nature but upon the power of its highest law. Therefore Christ was a mediator throughout the remarkable things he has done between the two factors which are forever most intimately united: scientific knowledge on the one hand and spiritual faith on the other. Only Jesus established a palpable truth: the supremacy of spiritual mind over physical matter.

Once more, the Garden of Eden was not the answer nor the Heavens above as Pope Paul said, as the secret dwelling of the Most High. Jesus provided that answer in straight and unconcealed manner: "God dwells within you." So "where" or "what" is that secret place is no more an inquiry. Yet we choose to settle in the same section of the mind that Jesus engage in and know we must not use the subconscious for any selfish reason but to arrive at the full unison with its Creator.

Our body is the Tabernacle of God or the House of the Lord. When He *restores our soul* or *renews our mind* then He dwells within us wholly. The subconscious is the portion made in the image of the Creator's mind, as recorded in Genesis. It is that portion of us that is the mind of God: an entity apart from anything earthly that makes its presence known only when the soul-self lifts itself into the vast, expansive level that is God and become a part of that oneness. In the following pages we cited many nomenclatures of the Father while classifying His many attributes. We relate to all these attributes by relating to Jesus Christ. Such specific relationship is what makes Christians different from the followers of other monolithic faiths and what distinctly shapes their approach to ethics, justice and peace. That is exactly what Paul meant when he said that Christians are supposed to be "in Christ," without really explaining how.

Subconscious in Psychology

"Imagination is everything. It is the preview of life's coming attractions."

Einstein

1900 years after Jesus pioneered the human subconscious mind psychological attempts rediscovered it and put it to many useful applications. Freud who was credited to trace its various characterizations gave it, along with his aficionados after him, the term *unconscious mind*. He made the breakthrough that many people acknowledged by simply identifying it. Carl Jung however, who went deeper in its examination preferred the *subconscious mind* which is also our preference. Yet Freud sensed another level in between that he called the *preconscious*. This polemic ended with the name *subconscious* as the ongoing one in much of the dynamic psychology literature.

These various levels of the subconscious can be easily detected. Yet the subconscious is more accessible as all its contents are personal whilst the unconscious, that features impersonal aspects of the mind collective to all humanity, is harder to penetrate. When scientists discovered the subconscious mind they were able to demonstrate the difference between the consciousness and the subconscious. The two minds have different qualities and abilities. The subconscious mind is very powerful and we have all experienced it knowingly or inadvertently every day of our lives. As we examine it further we perceive its untapped potential and the seemingly impossible things it easily does. For 6000 years—save the 3-year Jesus' ministry—we did not even know it existed, but just recently we have begun to understand its propensities.

We all know something about our mind. The term *mind power* and the subconscious mind power are felt in many different ways. In the psychosomatic sense mind power is labeled as ability to have emotions, imagination, memory, and will; while the subconscious mind power is identified as part of the normal individual personality in which mental processes function without consciousness even under normal waking conditions. Consciousness for most of us is our awareness of thinking, feeling, and performing. Although the reactions to the stimuli may differ from person to person or even in the same person from time to time; the fact that everyone is capable of reacting is taken as a sign of consciousness. Sometimes though, certain acts are performed reflexively or without conscious awareness. For instance mind goes on thinking bad thoughts despite attempts to control them; negative thoughts of anger, lust, jealousy, hatred and even desire to harm others; or opposite positive ones reflecting our good or noble feelings. These are the products of our dual internal power having its negative and positive currents. Our subconscious receives and records—or refuses and rejects them as dictated by our conscious mind.

We go in and out of the subconscious realm every day though most of the time we are not aware of it. When we daydream we are in that realm. Often a person will be staring out a window, thinking or dreaming of something, his mind can be thousands of miles away; then the telephone rings and his conscious mind wakes up, he may even jump a little from being startled. Driving a car takes such little conscious effort that we often daydream while driving, that is what I do all the time. If you have the radio on then your subconscious is open to its suggestions. If you need positive suggestions this is the best place and time to play a related CD because we naturally go then into the subjective realm or "twilight zone." When you first wake up in the morning and while still in bed, going in and out of sleep, is also a good time to give yourself some suggestions because you are under the spell of the subconscious realm. Did you ever go to sleep at night with a big problem on your mind? Well, your subconscious mind continued to work on the problem during the night while your conscious mind was sleeping. Then when it figured out the problem *it woke you up* and told you the answer. It's always a good idea to sleep on a major decision at least one night, so your subconscious can go to assimilate it for you. Try it the next time you have a problem. Think about it and tell your subconscious to figure it out then wake you when it has the answer. This is a time tested exercise, one that lets you access your subconscious.

The fact that many educated people blame their inner mind for some of the actions they take proves their awareness of it and their perception of its potentials. We need to bear in mind that while our subconscious can be our best friend it can also be our worst enemy since it is that forceful drive that essentially controls the life we live and underlines our personality. This *mind within your mind* is that little voice in the back of your head that you always hear when you are faced with a difficult situation. Its peculiar way of communication differs from one person to the next, meaning that no two people have the same type of subconscious interacting. Even if you were an identical twin and you were both raised in the same environment under the same conditions, you will both have a different inner voice.

A simple yet blatant example that can help understand the interaction with the subconscious is the process of breathing. Before you started reading the previous line, your breathing was controlled by your subconscious. If you try now and control your breathing differently by taking few deep intakes of air for one minute you will of course be able to do so. This time it was the conscious mind controlling your breathing, but when you let go of your intended pattern you are notified to be handing the task over to your subconscious mind.

There are many divergences between the two: the conscious mind goes to sleep at night but the subconscious never sleeps; in fact it has *never* been asleep for one single second in any human ever since he or she was a mere fetus. This is the tool that reflects our dreams when we sleep and the one that sustains the life functions of our body; it supervises our heartbeat, breathing or even eye blinking. The subconscious mind is in charge of *healing and repairing* the body.

Dr. George Pitzer sums up the mind-blowing powers of the subconscious as: "A distinct entity that occupies the whole human body and when not opposed in any way, it has absolute control over all the functions, conditions, and sensations of that body. While the objective (conscious) mind has control over all of our voluntary functions and motions, the subconscious mind controls all of the silent, involuntary, and vegetative functions. Nutrition, waste, all secretions and excretions, the action of the heart in the circulation of the blood, the lungs in respiration or breathing, all cell life, cell changes and development, are positively under the complete control of the subconscious. This was the only mind animal had before the evolution of the brain; and it could not, nor can it yet, reason inductively, but its power of deductive reasoning is perfect. It can *see* without the use of physical eyes. It perceives by intuition. It has the power to communicate with others without the aid of ordinary physical means. It can read the thoughts of others. It receives intelligence and transmits it to people afar. Distance offers no resistance to the successful missions of the subconscious mind."

It could be called the "feeling mind." This part of our brain seems like nothing more than a non-thinking, insensitive, machine-like brute; but is really an incredibly capable computer that never forgets. It does not care how much you hurt if you do. In fact the subconscious mind seems to view all emotions simply as its operating "facts"—just associated items in its database of information. It is only doing its job: constantly assimilating what has been *programmed* into it. Hence a human should be careful of what he or she chronicles in this computer because he or she would *sooner or later be getting to it.* Everything to the subconscious is cut and dried, black and white, and it will always give the same emotionally charged (plus or minus) answer to the same association until its programming or input is changed.

As new skills are learnt they too become programmed into our subconscious minds and rarely have to be thought of consciously again. These skills include things like learning to walk or to feed ourselves, riding a bicycle or driving a car. Once these skills have been learnt and programmed into your subconscious mind you no longer consciously require the knowledge for that particular skill or activity. It is a given exercise that you will be able to do again and it feels effortless—unlike the first time you ever tried it!

Without these subconscious programs the world would be a very different place. Your life would be affected dramatically and things that take you only a moment or two to complete would end up taking you hours. If you consciously had to think about every heart beat and every breath you take you would have very little time to fit anything else in. This is why the human mind is such a wonderful creation. Your subconscious mind is dealing with hundreds of different tasks simultaneously and this frees up the conscious mind for higher thinking and its role as the operator.

The subconscious is therefore comparable to a super computer where you can add and remove programs *at your will*. When you buy a new set it comes with a hardware equipped with an operating system which carries the necessary barebones that allows it to function: the box, the stored-in CPU, the monitor, keyboard and hard drive. Everything is there. Yet all this is worthless without the operating system: a set of codes or instructions that controls all the hardware on your system. Once it is installed the computer suddenly works and you can now use it for any of your purposes plus adding more programs to perform all sorts of functions. When you work out a task the computer is constantly sending electronic signals back and forth while using that software. *You are not conscious of it* though it is taking its course. Your subconscious power operates in the same way: your conscious mind or awareness is like text editing. You start typing your document on the screen, *conscious* of what to say and how to put in the right format and correct spelling. This is likened to the process of taking all the right decisions in your brain where the input is transferred to the subconscious or the hard disk you do not see in your computer. Once processed and stored there it constitutes your personal record containing your memories, habits and beliefs . . . your total personality. Your established belief systems express the way you live and act in your life; it simply reflects what you are, who you have been and who you will be in the future.

Our two basic constituents are the hardware and the software representing on the one hand the physical matter or body, and the bundle of thoughts, emotions, feelings, and complexes on the other. The body is more or less the same for everybody but the software is formed by the background, life history and experiences all different from one person to another. The software depends also on the different experiences in everybody's lives yet affects today's thoughts which come to two different persons on the same stimulation or in similar situations. The reactions are different because of the different thoughts that were unleashed. In this respect people have the same potential and are almost alike if dissociation between hardware and software is achieved. Yet software is deeply ingrained into the individual subconscious, tenacious and elusive to change. People look different by their genes and chromosomes but also by the constituents of their software. Yet if such constituents are *streamlined and rationalized within the positive path*, harmony and reconciliation would prevail among mankind: the basic philosophy of the Kingdom of God.

Comparing our inner mind to a computer means that whatever comes out depends on what is put in; the output depends on the input. Again, we have to be careful what to feed our subconscious : positive thoughts produce a positive life while negative ones lead to misfortunes. All thoughts produced by our conscious mind work in conjunction with our subconscious to produce our *habit patterns* which results we see in our lives; paying attention to what we feed is critical as this will mean the difference between success and failure.

The simplest way to understand the subconscious is as a sleeping mind that we are not mindful of. It is constantly recording new information we obtain from the environment around us and storing it away. Whatever we see, hear, smell, taste, touch or feel passes through the conscious mind and reaches the subconscious where it is then stored. This means that everything you have ever seen, heard or experienced has been filed away somewhere in the depths of your subconscious : a database providing for creativity or obliteration. Such influences impact each person and help form his/her belief systems when the person translates the influences of the unconscious into personal beliefs and attitudes that establish the strengths or weaknesses of his/her subconscious foundation.

It is totally undiscriminating and promiscuous. It welcomes every coincidence, every impression and every realization that rings its doorbell. It will not think over, think through or think twice—because it can't. It is the storehouse of all thoughts and feelings which together release electrical vibrations that, through the law of resonance or repetition, attract into people's experiences everything that resonates with their beliefs and convictions. Thus an observation made years ago is connected with a statement made two days ago and an idea based on this connection presents itself unexpectedly.

When it was discovered in the late 1800's hypnosis was demonstrated for the first time. Scientist's were able to put the conscious mind to sleep and then access the subconscious. First it was noticed that the hypnotized person was totally *amenable to suggestion*. That means he would *believe* whatever he was told. For example if he was told it was very cold he would begin to shiver. The room temperature could have been 90 degrees but if suggested it was cold he believed it. That is the *deductive reasoning*. The conscious mind reasons the exact opposite; it reasons inductively i.e. gathers facts then reasons up to a conclusion. The conscious mind *doubts* everything and must be convinced whilst the subconscious has perfect *faith* and never doubts when programmed with unwavering conviction and resolved will!

We have stated repetitively that God, the Father, or the Presence of Life dwells in our subconscious and His Spirit is what makes it function. This Divine Presence can be accentuated or minimized depending on how positive or negative we individually are. There are many similarities that suggest this consistency and the striking resemblance between the two is almost palpable: The mind of the Lord never sleeps and so does our subconscious; the mind of God reasons deductively and so does our subconscious; the First has perfect faith and that is exactly how our subconscious believes. When a human discovers his subconscious mind he is accessing to God. No human can log on his subconscious realm unless he uses the positive narrow door. *"Enter in at the strait (positive) gate;* Jesus said, *wide is the gate, and broad is the (negative) way that leads to destruction and many chose to take it. Because strait is the gate and narrow is the way which leads unto life, and **few are those who find it.***" (Mat. 7:13.)

While external hypnotism provides therapists access to your subconscious to awaken its potentials irrespective of how much negativity has accumulated in it through the years, self-hypnosis can delve deeper into the subconscious to cleanse its tares and implant positive seeds instead. This is the "born-again" process much highlighted throughout Jesus' philosophy. Today lots of people have experienced a great amount of good in their lives after achieving this transition into their positive realm. Some, who had tremendous self-doubt learnt to believe in their potentials and experienced a constant shower of success in their lives. This self-hypnosis is the best way to access the subconscious and calm a restless, hyperactive mind that is causing endless problems to its victim.

The time-tested theory is that when the pressures of the world close in one can simply enlist this nearby ally. Accessing your subconscious can be an easy exercise when you learn to allow yourself to enter the state of trance familiar to everyone: we all pass through this state as we go to sleep each night. We repeat that self-hypnosis is a natural state of mind between waking and sleeping either in the evening or in the morning. It is the time where your subconscious mind becomes open to new positive suggestions involving your desired change. Positive auto-suggestions addressed with belief are *Thought Forms* that will find their way to your subconscious tearing down the invisible walls of resistance.

Self-hypnosis or trance states are common whenever people focus their concentration. Our modern clerics deeply confined to their pigeonhole catechetic studies consider hypnotism an outright fallacy, let alone heresy. They experience like all of us some sort of hypnosis every day moments before and after their sleep. They dismiss the many instances in the bible where *God put a spell on* (to isolate the carnal mind) *and talk* to His chosen people in a dreamlike stupor. Apostle Paul accomplished this ability through intense devotion and described one instance of it in his own words: *"And it came to pass, that, when I was come again to Jerusalem, even while I prayed in the temple, I was in a trance"* (Act. 22:17.) The Greek meaning for *trance* or spell is to *displace the mind*. It is also translated as *amazement* or *astonishment*. But in any translation it implies the state of trance where the conscious mind is put to sleep or temporarily disabled. Modern self-hypnosis can be performed through relaxation ideally on a comfortable recliner with soft background music away from any interference. In this state of trance as well as the state of dozing to sleep or barely waking, you are what you think: your subconscious acts on all given thoughts and images and this is where your mind can *change its mind*. It has the full capacity to do that!

In hypnosis settings the practitioner personalizes specific suggestions according to his client's preferences and motivations. In self-hypnosis those preferences and motivations are directly injected into the subconscious. This learning and re-learning process requires patience, concentration and positive attitude. The subconscious does not respond to negative or harmful impulses for two distinct reasons: a/ such impulses are always accompanied with doubts, and b/ they do not fit into it initial positive programming. Accessing this realm can be through developing a positive mental-fitness program that addresses the particular situation of the individual and his or her specific needs and desires.

In this era of technology you may create your *subliminal messages* carrying your wants and aspirations and have them imbedded in your laptop to flash on your screen or listen to them on CDs while driving. These will be the *repeaters* that will echo their resonance frequently in your subconscious and serve as *follow-ups* for your mind manager to pursue until final fulfillment. You will not break any laws whenever these messages are strictly positive and for your personal use but you will however when you direct them negatively against others. Here you come into conflict with your subconscious which is by now programmed to deal with your ideal self. It is therefore important to look at your wants as goals and accomplishments yearning to be carried out and attained. This is the real job of your subconscious and your perseverance is the name of the game. Surely, problems and obstacles may arise but a smile can make short work of any difficulty. The important factor remains your faith that should stay steady as a rock.

I personally use self-hypnosis every night to induce myself to sleep and succeed, to the amazement of my wife, to start snoring within 10 minutes after hitting the pillow. This was my first entry into yoga world and actually some type of meditation. Later my hypnosis program focused on symptom management of pain, nausea and excessive appetite; creating a mood management to attain relaxation, optimism and specific imagery around various ailments to encourage the body's immune system to fight back. That was done without any self-evasion or mental reservation to match the black and white deductive reasoning of this amazing hidden machine.

A subconscious deductive reasoning means giving a picture of reality based on what has been programmed into it. It is not locked in time but has one window open to the present time and place and another to the infinity of all time and space. It is the filter between the finite and the infinite. Its position among the two levels gives it the unique capability to function as translator between the two. As such it seems to live in a sort of *spatial* time as opposed to the *linear* time of the conscious mind. Thus time to the subconscious seems to be irrelevant and therefore expandable or shrinkable according to its needs. It appears to exist in timelessness where the past is the same as now. However it can be programmed to recognize linear time very accurately.

Your mind power and your subconscious can jointly interact to fashion your *personal reality*. Power of the subconscious mind comes from the momentous thoughts and solemn beliefs of your mind's power. You can never trick your subconscious nor take it *on a trial basis*. Only what you genuinely think and firmly believe is what your subconscious mind power will stock up and later reproduce. This is done continuously one minute at a time. Every thought nourished resolutely by your mind power will activate your subconscious mind to generate those thoughts and energy whether good or bad into your life determining beyond any doubt the creation of your present and future.

Illustrating this process would help. It is similar to fertile soil that consents to any seed planted inside it. Your regular thoughts and beliefs are the seeds which are being planted and they will eventually produce their specific crop: weeds produce weeds and fruits generate fruits. You reap exactly what you plant. Your conscious mind is the gardener; its power is the path where you choose the kind of Thought Forms or seeds to be sown in your subconscious garden.

The subconscious is where *habits* nest and grow and it is as trainable as any domestic pet. It protects itself from change though with emotional—not analytical—responses. This is why whenever a person suddenly gets angry or emotional you can then tell where his *faith* lies. That can be anything from a scientific theory of evolution, to God's stature, down to simpler and mundane things. It is deeply ingrained and any force applied to it simply meets an equally forceful emotional response which is not necessarily logical but very, very powerful.

To wrap up a good understanding of our subconscious we should know that:

- *It develops the life force and power that enriches the soul.*
- *It has a perfect and complete memory of everything that has ever occurred to the body and mind combined.*
- *It accepts and is open to any type of suggestion from any source without judgment or awareness of right or wrong; it has no discrimination.*

- *It acts like a robot in doing exactly what it has been programmed to do by clear instructions from the conscious mind or society or outside suggestions*
- *Its complexes can be overridden with new programs if impacted sufficiently and persuaded to change.*
- *It overrides and betrays the logical, conscious mind if survival needs or logical desire patterns are threatened.*
- *It acts as a small devious child without discrimination or a sense of right or wrong.*
- *It creates strong fixations from linked traumas or emotional situations that it adheres to very strongly. (Like smoking or nail biting).*
- *It limits the conscious mind from evolving or accepting ideas which are contrary to its already programmed input.*
- *It understands violence, pleasure, trauma, enjoyment etc. but not their social or moral implications.*
- *It does not receive information from the conscious mind easily; only instructions with physical or symbolic nature or inputs with emotions and feelings are accepted.*
- *It expresses itself to the conscious with emotions, illness, feelings, images, dreams and body movements or even illogical actions.*

Our dreams are illogical expressions of our subconscious. They represent allegoric repetitions of our deep past or recent time memories and experiences. Many people have recurring dreams that usually represent subconscious attempts to resolve longstanding issues or solve problems that the dreamer faces in his or her waking life. Such dreams may point to an area of life that requires conscious attention and perhaps the implementation of changes. A recurring nightmare may represent an area of life that causes significant anxiety in the waking world.

Spirituality as we have seen can enhance healthiness through its positive channels. This is the "divine science" that makes the healing happen through the subconscious powers. A firm belief that inspires the faith in the individual and when supplemented by a parallel palliative suggestion it impregnates the subconscious to release and activate the infinite healing presence. This is a known truth that can change and save lives. Spiritual healing is based on the interactive union of the conscious and subconscious minds. Jesus used this method through the spoken word as well as the outer touch both powered by the Holy Spirit and his unshakable conviction that wholeness was a reality in everyone even when misperceived. The individual's subconscious will respond whether the object of faith is true or false though it is a rarity that a false objective injects true faith necessary for the action; the viruses of doubt are always there to agitate its very foundation.

This divine science has grown and thrived in recent years as a spiritual practice that has its doctors and ministers. Prominent among those is Dr. Jaime Cope who is a registered nurse as well. These spiritualists stress on the power of the mind and its dominance over the matter; a far cry from the early principles of the Essenes with whom Jesus spent what we call his *18 Lost Years*. Only they used a reverse order departing from *the laws of matter* to the *laws of mind* to *the laws of the Spirit* illustrating that mind and matter were meant to serve spirit. They believe Jesus understood the scientific *mind-body relationship* and the power of faith operating through the subconscious and manage to realize wholeness as a normative course.

Doctors now firmly believe that 75% of all diseases start in the mind. That's a very large amount; it means that 75% of all the people are sick today because they did not know how to use the power of their subconscious mind. If we feed this mind with positive thoughts of love, peace and joy we will enjoy a happy life. Positive thoughts protect us while negative ones such as hate, jealousy and anger act to help in destroying our bodies' immunity system and thus producing diseases. Throughout their lives individuals have been taught how to do everything but no one ever taught them how to use their mind. Only few learned how to harness, direct and instruct such hidden powers and begun to make use of them. Doctors will even tell you that most sickness and disease are caused by stress—which starts in the mind. They also say that we only use 10% of our mind power. It is like going through life spending 10-percent of your salary! Now imagine if we just used an additional 10% of our mind power correctly and how about using 90% of it? The results would be astounding! Reaching this high degree of utilization you will discover a new and amazing law of nature: *nothing is meant to be, nothing is written, you create everything.*

-7-

The Positive Recipient

"You are a nonstop creating machine; a manifesting maestro."

Mike Dooley

We are well versed by now with our internal power currents. Our conscious mind constantly reflects habitual thoughts; it is therefore *our responsibility* to influence this mind with positive emotions, thoughts and energy as dominating factors. Mind power is *creative* with positive thinking and *destructive* with negative thoughts. Unfortunately most of us lack the knowledge of this law and the psychology behind its manifestations. Because of this ignorance we have allowed all kinds of seeds both good and bad to enter our inner mind that will manifest in failure, ill health and all kinds of misfortunes just as effortlessly as it will exhibit success and abundance. As it cannot manifest it both at the same time we need to constantly actuate the positive until the fertile soil of the subconscious power reaps only abundance.

The old adage: "thinking is being" is so true because we *indeed are* what we think we are! If you think negative then negativity is what you ultimately get from the universe because the whole universe is in perfect balance of negative and positive vibrations. If you feel negatively about something, your subconscious immediately reflects it to the external universe. The micro is reflected in the macro and so you receive the negativity you release out. Conversely if you accost the positive path your subconscious is emitting positive vibes to the outside world and in return you receive positive experiences in life. This is the Law of Attractions that we will review in details.

In this context I remember a quartet of the great poet/philosopher Alma'ari in his poem addressing the human being:

> *"Your remedy is within you but you don't realize*
> *Your illness is from you but you fail to recognize*
> *You assume yourself a slight universal bit,*
> *But the Huge Universe dwells in this tiny size."*

We can consider the subconscious as our personal loggia wide open to the gigantic universe. Yet it is impartial in its correlations with the cosmos. It will just as readily disperse and glean negative sets of beliefs as well as positive ones. It is up to us to be the *gatekeeper* at the conscious mind to check the Thought Forms that enter and store up in the subconscious.

The more we monitor and become aware of our thoughts the more we control what enters and accumulates.

This extremely powerful tool we all have is hampered in most of us by our negative experiences that we just tend to resign to thinking that a life of incarceration is all we deserve so we learn to live with dissatisfying conditions. Negativity is Satan, the man-made human idol displaying our negative drift just waiting to get us in his grasp, while positivism is our angelic affinity. No matter how hard we try to remain cheerful our "Satan" would be right there patiently working out some strategy to get us down. By accosting the positive thinking corridor people can turn this tide to their advantage and swim on ahead in the knowledge that all would be set right soon. Here, it is important to remember that what a human wants to be is really all in his/her hands. Anybody who merely learns to think positively will see life transforming the right way and experience the best events of happiness, peace, prosperity, good health, great relationships, love and much more.

How to be practically positive? By simply spending some effort and time staying positive every day; this can be easily achieved when you cultivate in a daily fraction of the time your *positive self.* That does not mean that one has to be in a strained cheerful and enthusiastic mood all day long. Positive thinking simply means the absence of negative thoughts and emotions: the inner peace! When you are truly at peace within yourself you are naturally at peace with the larger universe engulfing you. You don't have to fight off negative thoughts or search desperately for more positive ones; it just happens naturally. Meditation can let go with the stressful or worrisome thoughts leading to relaxation of both mind and body.

A relaxed feeling will naturally lead to positive thinking that can and should be developed as a mental attitude. Pleasant feelings, constructive thoughts and images of our visualization can be a way of life. It brings brightness to the eyes, energy in the body and happiness to the soul. Its beneficial effect on health would be readily discernible. Positive thinking straightens our body language, the way we walk erect and the way we talk with power and confidence. It is contagious: our thinking affects what happens in the subconscious level by the transference of our thoughts and feelings to others, thus it readily interacts with other people and motivates them to help and be friendly, or, to avoid us if we are negative. This power of thought is a big and dangerous weapon; it shapes our life that is done subconsciously though achieved through the conscious corridor. Yet, entertaining positive thoughts, ideas, beliefs, and faith is not an easy job; it should be practiced with a genuine desire, selfless yearning and above all, absolute perseverance, persistence and determination. We should constantly use affirmations expressed with positive words to improve our thinking.

What are affirmations? They are simple but consequential statements used in a positive present tense language. They serve to prompt and ascertain the subconscious—that cannot be tricked—of our absolute determination. If good health is your goal for instance frame a sentence to present tense "I am healthy" or "I am on my way to good health". These power affirmation words have their strong impact on the subconscious motivation. Norman Peale used to affirm himself with these words: "Every day, in every way, I'm getting better, better and better"; this was his self-assertion of the task entrusted to his subconscious.

This affirmation power works for us because we feel good when we say it even if we still have room for improvement. "I am" is very powerful and binds us with whatever we say after.

Jesus' repetitive "I am" affirmations disparaged by ignorant laymen as showy and pretentious were his examples for all of us to pursue. *"I am the living bread;" "I am from above;" "I am the light of the world;" "I am the good shepherd;" "I am the resurrection and the life;"* and, *"I am the way, the truth, and the life."* Such assertions were not only meant to reinforce his already unshaken belief but to inject that kind of belief in his disciples and listeners. Furthermore, he constantly thanked God for this empowerment and set an equal pattern for us to copy. These *Thank You* notes to the Divine serve to feel gratitude now and in the future of the absolute outcome our faith and confidence will bring forth: the manifestations of our wants and wishes.

Positive thinking is a mind healing process when supported by affirmations and visualizations. Skeptics claim it does not help with the real problems nor does it lead to palpable manifestations. This is very true as far as those skeptics are concerned and it happens most of the time to those of meager faith. Solid affirmations can be used to solve the emotional negativity brought by a biased balance between positive and negative understandings at the conscious level. The emotional understanding toward situations usually helps and has little to do with intellectual capacity. What counts here is the emotional balance while confronting situations where chances for success and happiness are definitely sustained by this approach.

Others may overvalue negative aspects as a way to protect themselves against feared situations. Their intellectual understanding may tell it does not make sense at all but for some unknown reasons they act and feel upon unreal negativity. For them the dominant part of their mind make-up is negativity towards certain situations. Of course, the use of positive thinking affirmations helps them for a healthier balance between their opposing currents to understand life at conscious and emotional levels. Very seldom this look at life will cause them to replace all negative understandings for positive ones. They just learn to open up to more positive situations that can be expected for them. The large majority of them will never deny evident negative experiences of real practice for the sake of it alone.

The subconscious being a positive as well as negative recipient catalyst can only be influenced through positive affirmations in order to create a healthy balance in the inner self. Again, positive affirmations have the effect of achieving a more balanced understanding thus allowing the person to understand situations and adapt to them in a more realistic way. Positive affirmations create a healing similar in some ways to a rewiring process. Repetitive affirmations create a resonance that occurs as a healing process more consistent with reality. The effects will be the same even if you even use "unrealistic affirmations" when these are injected with a certain degree of belief, leading further to a healthier balance.

"I can do this," *"I will do this,"* *"I will be happy"* etc. Are positive affirmations that help the subconscious to nurture and process our wants and desires into palpable outcomes. Often we tend to act in a particular way without our knowledge as most of our behavior is governed by this amazing machine. The positive thought process in the subconscious achieves positive thoughts in the conscious state; hence the importance of allowing only positive words, ideas and thoughts to consciously enter our subconscious realm. This may seem to the novice *easier said than done* because most of the times we revert back to our self-doubt, fear of failure, pain, grief etc. Such vulnerabilities however will dissipate when we strongly and firmly believe in ourselves. Jesus told us if we garner belief the size of a grain we would move mountains. He believed in what he said, accomplished miracles, and assured us that: *"greater works you will accomplish when you believe."*

Through countless centuries humanity has been told that it is inherently evil, doomed and basically not worth the price of its human stature. Jesus came to reverse this cycle and activate the positive *angelical powers* of humankind by ushering in the Kingdom of God. His *greatly misinterpreted* message has been so twisted that humanity is of the belief that its existence is at the whim of some vengeful god that will probably destroy the whole creation being essentially worthless. Jesus humanized this god calling Him Father and elevated man to the divine stature. Yet we have been reminded repeatedly that we are in need of salvation because there is a great evil force in the world and that we are under its control. If we are fortunate and follow the rules of established churches—and mosques—, there is a slim chance that we may not burn for eternity for our woe begotten ways. Under such inherited postulates you need not ask why people have such a wavering belief in creating their new reality.

None of this is new. Mystics have long held that we do in fact control our distinctiveness; not just the little things in life but everything. They have maintained that regardless of our circumstances each person has the innate, universal potential or Father and that given ability to create or alter at our will. Skeptics keep saying that we are here to suffer or to live a life of misery while each conflict or problem that we confront is merely an opportunity to express our *higher selves* to our liking. They claim there is only a God who seeks to punish and that the further steps are to end in doom. This concept makes no sense if you understand that we can live an elevated life evolving to a higher state of being: the state of partnership with the Father.

Most psychologists today believe that people have the ability to create and control such things as health, abundance, relationships and literally every aspect of their being. Many of them deliberate over the matter of reciting positive affirmations as the key to reconcile the two aspects of our minds. Almost all of them agree that the issue is a mere positive thinking. In order to truly take conscientious control of our life it is necessary to change our vibratory nature and utilize the laws of physics to *attract* what we want to change, bring into or remove from our lives. The notion of quantum physics says the entire universe that includes us is *vibratory* in nature and when people truly vibrate positive thinking they literally attract positive aspects into their lives. The upcoming pages will hopefully carry tangible proof as to how this process works.

Accessing
the Subconscious

"All truths are easy to understand once they are discovered; the point is to discover them"

Galileo

F ar from any kind of religious belief, science today teaches people of various upbringings and cultures how to tackle the powers of their subconscious. They simply differentiate the two parts of the mind: the one that we are aware of and the powerful, latent subconscious that handles—

processes—thousands of things every minute and constitutes the real power of creativity. This power emanates from all those things you are not aware of—memories you don't remember, things you have seen but have not noticed and feelings within you that naturally occurred. In fact all of your new great ideas are lying inside there right now. The trick is in figuring out how to access them.

You cannot achieve this access by thinking because once you start to think you are back to the confines of the conscious that may produce one or two ideas that will not lead to the sublime moment you are looking for. The intensity of using the conscious mind, *your carnal mind*, blocks your ability to access your subconscious. It creates a turbulent and restless subconscious unable to respond. Hence the important technique in keeping that mind quiet and still; you will then communicate with it and hear what is telling you.

This is likened to a pond of water; you throw a pebble into it and if it is calm the pebble creates clearly visible ripples. If turbulent, any ripples are hidden amongst the churning waters. When you are calm, your mind, like the still pond, is equally quiet. The pebble is a question or problem you have. When you pose this question to your still mind your subconscious creates possible answers/ripples, and you can actually *see* all the solutions your mind is giving you. The turbulent pond on the other hand is your mind going wild with myriads of thoughts and your thrown questions are lost amid the turbulence. Meditation as we have seen is one way to calm your mind when you spend some quiet time alone at home or in nature. Another is exercise that could be either spiritual such as prayer or physic-spiritual like yoga. When your mind is free from interference and calm like a pond access to your subconscious becomes effortless.

While attempting this access one should not be shy, fearful or reserved. It should be taken as meeting a new friend to establish an intimate and lasting relationship that would transcend belief systems and cumulative habits. Through this intimacy all negative addictions that have been ingrained for years shall be adjusted and or, eventually eliminated. Your shyness or hesitation to establish this access shall simply be subdued through good will and constant practice.

This direct and intimate accessing can be a powerful yet jovial exercise. Think of your subconscious not as impenetrable mazes but rather a trainable dog though it is more powerful and sneaky than your conscious mind. Should there be a conflict between your conscious and subconscious the latter will win every time: the former is flexible and compliant, the latter is programmed and rigid. Have you ever done something and afterward wondered: what was I thinking? Your subconscious could answer that question for you. It holds all the programming, learning, habits and garbage that you have piled up across the years and any of it can wash up unexpectedly in your day to day activities.

A simple yet important exercise will help you experience your contact with your giant pet and strengthen your belief in its power: select a sleepy state where your mental efforts are reduced and your mind not as prevalent. Your negative thoughts are now suppressed and your subconscious is amenable. Pick a simple habit you want to get rid of (smoking, nail biting . . .) and compose a phrase: "I am now free of (your habit)". Keep repeating it over and over slowly, calmly and *faithfully* (you cannot trick your subconscious) for 5 minutes every time you wake up or go to sleep for a few days. Repetition (resonance) would be accepted as a *genuine demand* by your subconscious and *it will* free you from your habit. The repetition adds *emotion* to your statement each and every time and will lead to changing the former programming forever. In this exercise you have used your brain frequencies to a heightened emotional state that would spur your abilities in all areas of life. Higher frequencies are always attached to positive thoughts and feelings; they always pave the way to accessing your subconscious. This elementary exercise is only the beginning to your greater feats later depending only on your belief and dedication.

———◇———

Approaching the imagery of the subconscious is a technique that works best with simple people—*blessed are the meek*—. These are the people who don't have highly analytical minds who act like innocent children free of any negative brain waves. It is a learned skill that improves with constant practice. The lucid visuals of the imagery in the subconscious can best be compared to the lucidity of the dreams it reflects in our sleep. Most of it however runs in a stealth mode with a filter between the conscious and the subconscious preventing this fluency. Catching this fleeting stealth mode however gives us the effect of being in control instead of being controlled. This can be achieved when we reach into the dream state without having to fall asleep: a midway between the conscious being slowly disconnected and the subconscious gradually taking over. At those close-up moments you may start your visualizations like any daydream with the same purity of a little child where your eyes are closed and your mind taking you off on those tangents of thought. Keep up this state of visualizations without being pulled back into the conscious mind. Practice alone would keep in this state of "trance" where your *self* slips out of the conscience into the subconscious. You are now in constant touch with that mind where you may talk and dictate your wants and wishes. This experiment would put you face to face with your subconscious; it would stimulate your positive human self and helps you understand it and evaluate it.

Our subconscious is the gateway to the *Creative Level of Mind*. When you access this level you also access the *Creativity sector* where our inspired intentions (thoughts; feelings; desires; and belief systems) are being processed then carried out towards manifestation. This optimal and creative state of mind occurs when accessed and motivated under proper mental conditions, physically and emotionally, where the analytical consciousness fades to the background.

In the normal waking state this *Creative Level's* potential is nowhere near peak efficiency because during this state the subconscious is extremely busy processing all inputs of our five senses. This marvelous machine is also busy breathing for us, circulating blood through our system and carrying out an endless inventory of bodily functions in addition to all our habitual patterns of behavior. Consequently, both our conscious and subconscious are hard at work during the wakeful state and our awareness is literally scattered in order to deal with the many challenges of daily life. To reach that optimal, transitory state of relaxed mind and inject successful creation we have to resort to contemplative relaxation.

Once access is established we acquire the unmistakable feeling that we are sitting with a friend and confident to whom we can start messaging our creative intentions. Yet within this simple and gracious companion *lies the formidable power behind all creation*. It is the energetic universal force that vibrates the creative particles and the catalyst that causes all movement in the Universe. Its omnipresence pervades all creations and is perfectly interconnected with each creative particle as well as each mind throughout the Universe. Even the very movement of your hand and the growing of your hair are parts of this creative power in action. Jesus called it Father and revealed that *"even the hairs of your heads are counted."*

This is indeed *the Father* of all Creation, the Power of God that is given several other names and characterizations. Whatever we might choose to call it, make no mistake: it is the energetic might behind all Creation and the power that responds intelligently to our positive perception.

The existence of this power makes all things possible. While everyone is aware of it at various levels few are sentient of their inextricable connection to this power. Yet we are immersed in it exactly as fish in water. Most of the time we do nothing to derive further power from it although through our awareness its creative forces constitute our living capabilities. It is the ambient power of the universe in which we dwell and all things that represent the universal energy in action. The plain truth is that the majority of people are using it unconsciously; accessing the subconscious to derive a parcel of the remaining 90% of this dormant energy would surely spur the human being to further spiritual dimensions.

And as we said repeatedly: You cannot trick your subconscious; it is the voice of God emanating from within you. Therefore when you pull off the right of entry into it you can feel it immediately as a joyful wave of exhilaration. What we regard as trial and error experiments in our attempts we could perhaps minimize as we learn to log on repetitively until we feel it. We may need to oscillate between the two minds until we discover the vast creative energy/intelligence that exists in the subconscious realm.

—————◆⬦◆—————

Tackling the hidden powers of the subconscious may be a new experience to many. Those enthusiasts should therefore guard against taking the concept too far. They may not be sure whether the outcome will move them closer to their life-purpose or further away. It has taken mankind millions of years before Jesus Christ made people evolve to a state where we are aware of a mind that can be trained to work for us. This knowledge evaporated after his Ascension to be rediscovered by science a couple of hundred years ago. Jesus started it all using the positive approach embodied in the holy spirit of God and achieved miracles both in his own body and those of other humans. He warned us of the dangers when negative state is acted upon where untold misery can follow. It remains today a rewarding experience when people buy into this concept of training the mind to be as positive and objective as possible.

Hence the subconscious mind vast and non-discretionary as it is can be a powerful tool for creation or destruction. It is a wonderful machine when positively used to provide information and aid the conscious mind in accomplishing its quests. It is mature and evolved enough to handle the responsibility of being a guide to the conscious mind and assume its tremendous responsibility to convey messages from the spirit. A positive thought is always discernable: it is made out of love and aligned with the spirit; a message of how to love ourselves and others better that is readily and correctly interpreted.

Jesus may not have been the first prophet of love but surely the first to promulgate universal love that raises our state of consciousness to experience that we are all one in this universe. At this sublime level we are able to access the subconscious whenever we seek it. There will be no doubt in our minds regarding what the message is. It may not make logical sense to the conscious mind and it may even cause unhappiness. However a message aligned with the spirit is not related transient happiness or sorrow but part of our overall spiritual mission.

It requires lots of courage to approach that inner mind. A move totally supported by belief and a prayer fostered by emotions. Jesus warned of disbelief. When Peter failed to walk few steps on water to meet him and started sinking he scorned him: "Why did you doubt?" Our doubts are signs of a less evolved relationship with our whole self and an inner conflict that exhibits anger, hate, frustration, fear, loneliness and a myriad of countless negative feelings. They render the mastery of the subconscious impossible and our indoctrination futile: all our requests would be rebuffed then surface back to our consciousness as "unanswered prayers".

The Spiritual Law
of Attraction

*"Do not judge, and you will not be judged. Do
not condemn, and you will not be condemned.
Forgive, and you will be forgiven. Whatever you
want others to do for you, do so for them, for*
<u>*this is the Law*</u>*."*

Jesus

N ot too long ago I was cautious in tackling the subjects
of this book especially the Law of Attraction, let
alone publishing them. The "New Age Nonsense"

that is still despised by common thinkers was pushing me away from being among the few "wise ones" who could see through the smoke and *fool* the others. Even when I ventured my previous book "Jesus Christ that Unknown" many were dubious and distant. My skepticism phased out to conviction slowly but surely while dwelling deeper in Jesus' teachings and deciphering their hidden meanings. One issue was surfacing in my mind all along: do we reach our full potential by accepting the current beliefs? Or shall we pull ourselves out of skepticism and adopt ideas that usher in a new avenue of promise, power and hope that Jesus incited us to by *knowing the truth that will liberate us?*

This Law of nature is a sowing and reaping operation and like all Universal Laws; extremely important to understand and implement whether we are the kind that attracts the things we most desire or repel those we do not desire. It is immutable and unwavering; it cannot be changed or manipulated and furthermore it constantly functions and never rests. In this aspect it is comparable to the subconscious mind in the human being that never sleeps one single moment throughout the entire lifespan. Like all laws of nature it has existed since the beginning of time and will continue into infinity. It is not subject to adjustment like the subconscious that constitutes the only corridor to its vast potentials. The Law of Attraction operates methodically, flawlessly and consistently irrespective of one's awareness or ignorance of it.

This much pursued Law through Jesus' parables and connotations as we shall see, has been recently the cherished *discovery* of psychologists and psycho-spiritual essayers like me. It has been given alternative appellations: The Power of Intention, the Law of Abundance, the Secret, the Biology of Belief, the Creative Visualization, the Science of Deliberate

Creation, the Quantum Law of Attraction and many more . . . So, what is the Law of Attraction?

In its quantum physical aspect it is the magnetic power of the Universe to pull or attract similar energies together. It manifests in numerous, gravitational ways. The law of gravity of the earth is one of the examples. Another is the giant cosmic attraction structure that helps keep celestial bodies in their prescribed paths. This same law also affects on a smaller scale all human beings in their thoughts, ideas, situations, circumstances etc. The Law of Attraction stipulates that you attract into your life *whatever you think about.* Your dominant thoughts will find a way to manifest. Among human beings it attracts people with similar ideas, views, thoughts, perceptions and perspectives. Hence the popular adage: *birds of the same feather flock together.* But the Law of Attraction gives rise to some tough, heretofore unanswered questions none of them caused by the Law itself but rather through its application to objective reality.

Let us now take a closer scientific look at this law. Anything you can physically experience with the human senses consists of subatomic structures known as particles referred to as energy or vibration. In the same way the unseen things that cannot be attained by the senses such as the *thoughts you emit*, the oxygen you breath etc. are also when analyzed, vibration or energy. In the intangible world the scientific community states: The Law of Attraction is the law by which *a thought correlates with its object.* A palpable example in a more physical perspective is when we use two eye droppers one containing oil and the other water. We release a drop of water on a surface and on top of it an oil drop: drops separate from each other . . . one repels the other . . . though they are a liquid substance they don't mesh together into one mass. Only when we release a drop of water over water or oil over oil the cohesion happens. This is how the Law of attraction works. Although oil and water are both liquid each has individual subatomic constituent which is different from the other. Since they vibrate at different frequencies they are unable to be attracted to each other; different subatomic structures discharge different energy frequency. If we continue our experiment and release two drops of water (or oil) one on top of the other we see them meshing in one big drop because their rates of vibration are individually the same: related vibrations of energy "harmonize" and attract other similar frequencies.

This Law works constantly in everybody's life. People do not feel its presence while though they are completely immersed in it. The fish cannot alter the water's substance but humans can now transform this hidden force for their bliss or doom depending on how positive or negative they think. "*The Law of Attraction,* said Joseph Murphy, *attracts to you everything you need according to the nature of your thoughts. Your environment and personal conditions are the perfect reflection of your habitual thinking.*" This force can be compared to gravity or better still, to the moving wind. Jesus used this association in explaining the spiritual renaissance to Nicodemus but the Jewish cleric could not grasp it: "*Marvel not that I said unto you, you must be born again. The wind blows where it lists, and you hear the sound thereof, but cannot tell whence it comes and whither it goes: so is everyone that is born of the spirit . . .*" (John 3:3.) What Jesus tried to explain to Nicodemus in our modern terms is the true personality of each "*born again*" (who achieved personal subconscious cleansing) with all the positive requisites to enter the Kingdom of God. Such personality carries an ethereal, glorified body governed and directed by the spirit, the holy spirit of God that moves about like the wind! The Law of Attraction is just the same. You don't really *see* it but you know it exists.

This Law can be your friend or foe. It is the cosmic force directly linked to your subconscious and sharing with it many similarities: it really doesn't care what hurts or pleases you. It works like an independent, well oiled machine or a perfect computer program. Yet it won't do you any good or bad unless you tackle that machine or activate that program. When we dream, whether night or day, we fantasize about our goals, wishes and wants. There and then we are using the Law of Attraction and we glean whatever response from it depending of our *forceful determination* that we usually call "intense prayer".

Contemporary writers who tackled this Law adopted a purely psychological approach with a distinct aim: making money and attaining wealth. The purpose behind this exercise is to target the needy and fortune seekers thus ensuring larger sales of their books. A case in point is Napoleon Hill the author of: "Think and Grow Rich". He sold 60 million copies in the US discussing the importance of controlling thoughts in order to achieve wealth. He dubbed it *the secret* to success and described in each chapter the *energy* human thoughts have and their ability to attract other thoughts. Hill did not refer directly to the Law of Attraction but hovered around it mentioning the *vibratory power* of human thinking. He did not go through the subconscious as the catalyst providing functionality to the intentions and directing them towards manifestation. His work is comparable to the children's intentions when their mind is set on them: Their innate subconscious directs their burgeoning entities into fulfillment.

Most modern advocates of this Law succumb to the same error. They relate all solely to consciousness that represent to them a subjective reality in every human. They do not recognize that a human is a mere conscious body walking around in a world full of unconscious automations; which is a total misunderstanding of the subjective reality. The correct viewpoint is that consciousness is directly connected to the subconscious where this entire reality takes place. You know this is how your dreams work; your waking reality is just another type of dream and both types are the products of your subconscious. Physical reality works the same way as dreaming although it is a denser universe than what you experience in your sleeping dreams. Changes occur a bit more gradually here but reality still conforms to your thoughts just like a sleeping dream; your intentions are your projections that your subconscious will grab to assimilate and work toward their fulfillment.

Thought Forms are our moving vehicles to transform this life. Hence the need to avoid planting "weeds" and deal with those already there and dispose of them when we simultaneously mature with them, providing a nurturing space for the positive thoughts to strive and bear fruits. This is the core of the Law of Attraction that Jesus established and disseminated. Hence we should remember that when:

> *We sow a thought;*
> *We reap an action.*
> *We sow an action;*
> *We reap a habit.*
> *We sow a habit;*
> *We reap a character.*
> *We sow a character,*
> *We reap a destiny.*

Today, there is nothing mysterious or *secret* about the Law of Attraction nor is it difficult to understand as many visualize. Becoming aware of and learning how to harmonize with it is a simple matter when taking the first step to access the subconscious and acquire a basic understanding of how to make it work consistently. No individual can hide from the Law of Attraction or escape its effects yet anybody can control it when consciously exercising a free will request backed by an intense (vibratory) desire. The intensity of *giving out* to it determines what you shall *receive in return*. In this context one must first learn to consciously align all thoughts, beliefs and emotions with the desired outcome which will with unwavering belief allow you to attract whatever is desired. By the same token when one unleashes negative thoughts and emotions of fear, anxiety, lack, limitation, etc. one can only expect to attract more of the same.

When we change our thoughts we will change our beliefs and our whole world. Everything that is coming into our life is attracted by virtue of the images we are holding in our mind. Positive thinking generates motivation; the opposite is true within the negative arena. Our thoughts have wings that take them anywhere in our universe. Each one of us is *a human transmission tower* more powerful than any television tower created on earth and far different being also *a reception station*; a transmission tower that reaches the cosmos to create our life and shape our world. The frequencies we emit transcend distances and penetrate thick walls. They reverberate throughout the entire universe carrying the intonations of our thoughts!

In this respect connoisseurs in this knowledge marvel at the ignorance of most people who diffuse venomous thoughts against their peers and acquaintances while giving them cheap friendly talk. Such people are completely unaware of the verifiability of their thoughts and emotions and naive as to the unwavering and predictable operation of the Law of Attraction. "Nothing hidden that shall not be exposed and nothing concealed that shall not be revealed" said the Master. Those moving human transmission/reception towers keep diffusing and catching messages day and night to/from their many associates within the ambient human mantle. This extrasensory perception overtly known as the sixth sense is a major constituent of the Law of Attraction. No one therefore can deceive anyone with his feelings or emotions: both true and faked thoughts are instantly deciphered; the negative breeds negative and the positive triggers positive; hence the continuous replication in this book to control personal thoughts.

While there is absolutely nothing wrong about positive thinking we wonder sometimes, due lack of belief, why it does not have that much effect on the long run. The reason is obvious: positive thinking deals with a mere 10% of our conscious awareness. The larger, untapped mind space is now accessible to our testimonials of positive thinking that is harbored by our subconscious. The limited conscious space we dwell into to plant our seeds is floundered by deductive thinking that yearns for full assurance. Our good seeds there are in continuous conflict with the innate seeds of doubt that block the way to a subconscious acceptance. Faith however, both in the subconscious powers and the infinite capabilities of the Law of Attraction, will lead us to results unlike anything else that we may have read or seen.

The spiritual facet of the Law of Attraction reveals how to consciously, purposefully and consistently utilize it to attract the desired outcomes in EVERY area of your life physically, relationally, emotionally and spiritually. Its spiritual aspects further support its existence and help skeptics in validating its *truth*.

Science has made *incredible strides* in the past few hundred years to understanding how events and circumstances in human life come into physical existence. Numerous ancient texts have defined in amazing details what science is just coming around to understand through conventional methods. The great spiritual writings that have been uncovered throughout history talk about this phenomenon. Although only recently the Law of Attraction was given its current name it existed since the beginning of time! While psychologists introduced it as the *"the law by which <u>thought</u> correlates with its object,"* the Great Nazarene brought it closer to the existing level of comprehension in his time when he said: *"Whatsoever things you desire when ye pray, <u>believe</u> that you receive them and you shall have them."* Jesus established through this saying that belief begins as a thought attached to—and intensified by emotion which creates and bolsters faith.

You may lean on the scientific definition or chose Jesus' spiritual one, your understanding will be evident that both depict the Law of Attraction. Jesus however, established that a combination of thought, emotion and belief creates an intensified frequency that attracts additional vibrations or energy of a harmonious frequency. The result is that what you believe is manifest in the physical sphere; the more the intensity of your emotion, the higher the vibrations and the more forceful the frequency carrying your message. Jesus gave us a blatant display of that reality when he prayed in Gethsemane. Of the many aspects of his initial suffering the one of particular physiological interest is the bloody sweat. Interestingly enough, the physician Luke was the eye-witness evangelist who competently described this incidence: *"And being in an agony (intense devotion), he prayed the longer. And his sweat became as drops of blood, trickling down upon the ground."* (Luk. 22:44.) Jesus prayed intensely, sending irrevocable and final vibratory plea to perform his mother of miracles: the Resurrection.

It is important to notice that Jesus said *whatsoever you believe* not just this or that but *anything* you believe. Intense prayer can bring out miraculous results. Another Jesus' stipulation: *"I tell you the truth, if you have faith as small as a mustard seed, you can say to this mountain, 'Move from here to there' and it will move. Nothing will be impossible for you."* Again, he doesn't say except for this or that; faith results from a belief that begun as a thought. Here we also note his confirmation: *nothing will be impossible.* Prayer with belief activates that latent energy within us and generates a surge of *divine power* that *can remove mountains*, irrespective what the mountains are: a physical disability, a broken relationship, a career problem? In reclaiming your Spiritual Power you can confront that mountain knowing you have the authority to do it and knowing that something will follow.

The Law of Attraction was very much in display when the sick lady touched his garment and got healed: *"I felt a Power (electrical) getting out of me"*. He truly lost part of the power accumulated in his human body and *perceived* it instantly. It was caused by the persistent, vibratory and silent plea sent by the woman who *believed* that *only if I could touch his garment I would be whole.* Her belief which began as a vibratory thought stopped her suffering. Jesus told her: *Daughter, your faith has healed you. Go in peace and be freed from your suffering.* He did not say: I have healed you, but rather "your faith has healed you."

Here is the big difference between the scientific approach to the Law of Attraction and the spiritual one. Faith, or belief, is the single most important ingredient in the whole process. Belief alienated from spirituality is a shaky one haunted always by the conscious vacillations. True knowledge isn't about intellect as much as it is about spirit; the spirit will show the tremendous power available when you really approach it on an intimate level. It is the spiritual ignition that lies in the subconscious of every human waiting to be instructed with unshakable belief to perform miracles. The Old Testament equally abounds with testimonials of true faith being: "the substance of things *hoped for*, the evidence of things *not seen*." Which meshes well with contemporary psychological stipulations that thought develops belief as it "correlates with its object to make it manifest in the physical." The Bible also said: "As a man *thinks, so is he*," Or, whatever your thoughts consist of they create and display your reality.

Although Jesus promoted the Law of Attraction both within human relationships *(Judge not, that you be not judged. For with the judgment that you pronounce you will be judged.)* and people's beliefs that shapes their lives' predicaments; many Christians wonder today if practicing this Law contradicts their spirituality. In fact the Law meshes palpably with the basic Christian principles where faith comes first and foremost: The firm belief in knowing that what you want shall be yours the moment you ask and that the entire universe shifts to bring it into the blatant result. Jesus taught those who "have ears to listen" that we must act, speak, and think as if we are receiving now and that the Universe (note the capital U), or "Father" is a mirror and the Law of Attraction is mirroring back to us our dominant thoughts (relayed through intense prayers).

Christianity recognizes the power of faith to bring about positive changes not merely as an internal motivator but also as an external creative energy: *"Ask and you shall receive."* Jesus taught this Law in the parables when he asked us to believe and said that we could perform miracles just as he did. If you look at this with the Law in mind it would seem that in the stories of Jesus he even down played the miracles in the people around him by offering them the gift of strong belief; when we understand this we realize they actually healed themselves.

The elements were the cornerstone in his philosophy; he further commended wisdom and perseverance when *sowing* our thought/seeds and waiting for their fruition and He treated *delayed manifestation* as a symptom we have to act on and remedy its causes rather than getting impatient and disillusioned with the Law the way it became known to us today. He taught to realize and accept that due to the very nature of what we call physical reality there will very often be a delay in experiencing the desire in physical reality due in part to our low vibration in dealing with the physical Universe. He knew these truths very well and taught them in several parables, particularly this one:

"A certain man had a fig tree planted in his vineyard; and he came and sought fruit thereon, and found none. Then said he unto the dresser of his vineyard, behold, these three years I come seeking fruit on this fig tree, and find none: cut it down; why cumbers it the ground? And he answering said unto him, Lord, let it alone this year also, till I shall dig about it, and dung it: And if it bear fruit, well: and if not, then after that you shall cut it down." (Luk. 13:6)

The fig tree, is a metaphor for a partially developed Thought Form that has not yet come to fruition. The owner of the vineyard was upset because the tree was occupying space (our mental preoccupation) without producing any fruit. He was being much too impatient but the vineyard dresser (his conscious wisdom) knew of course that with the right nurturing and attention the fig tree would bear fruit (manifestation of our desires.)

The lesson is that once you have created your Thought Form intentionally and commit it through your subconscious to the Law of Attraction it should not be abandoned for slow fruition though it exists. But once nurtured and fertilized with the right impulses, expectations, feelings and above all *True Faith*, fruition will come through with the God-given universal powers of creation.

This creation continues every minute of every day. There is *absolutely nothing* that can stop it from being so. Exactly as the grass continues to grow when we sleep so does the work of our subconscious mind with all that was indoctrinated through our steadfast belief. Our wants and desires can only be thwarted by a conflicting subconscious, stirred by negative emotions that are not aligned with our well defined desires. These are the seeds of doubt that develop negative consequences usually referred to as "unrequited prayers." The Scripture is full of warnings to those with shaky belief. Among his disciples, it looks like Paul was about the only one who caught the message of the Master. In his epistle to the Hebrews he warned: *"So do not throw away your confidence; it will be richly rewarded. All you have need of is patience, that after you have done the (positive) will of God you will receive what he has promised."* (Heb. 10:35.)

Let us repeat: on the one hand the physical Universe is at the very extreme of vibration and a much slower rate with their higher density than the inner worlds; thus it apparently takes so *long* to display a desire: on the other hand the subconscious, transmitter of the Thought Forms, takes time to assimilate and accept the true wishes and intentions that can only be solidified by the only process known to both psychology and spirituality: repetitive affirmation.

-10-

Subconscious in Human Life

"Your life is a mirror of your consistent thoughts."
Napoleon Hill

As we often replicated in this book, becoming aware of the subconscious means acquiring the mastery of all behavioral characteristics and paving the way to human bliss and beatitude. Andrew Carnegie, the famous American sociologist says: "I am no longer cursed by poverty because I took possession of my own subconscious and that mind has yielded me every material thing I want and much more than I need. This power of mind is a universal one available to the humblest person as it is to the greatest." Taking charge of our subconscious leads us to change our lifestyles by holding our life's directions in our hands. This inner mind is the vehicle invoking the Law of Attraction to treat and realize our desires and eliminate countless malaises of our daily lives. Having read so far I know you still have the persistent question: How can I change my life around with the use of positive thinking?

The answer is simple: by changing the style and composition of your thinking and feeling. Waldo Emerson puts this change in an easy and simplified format: "actions and feelings go together. If we can control the actions that we can, we could then control the feeling that otherwise we cannot." A perceptible application: You wake up one morning and find yourself depressed (feeling). Start singing (you may have to force it first) your favorite and funniest song (action). As you gradually indulge in singing, gradually as well you feel your depression dissipate. Once you bring yourself back to happy and positive thoughts you can then influence your state of mind and interact once more with your subconscious.

Similarly to the connection between actions and feelings there is a strong connection between our body and mind. If we *choose* to live a healthy and happy life our conscious mind will transfer our wish to the subconscious to act on it day and night. Here we see how important is our awareness of how our subconscious operates with either positive or negative impulses; this magnificent and powerful machine will then work for our success or doom. I know I am being repetitive on these points; the objective is to stress to you personally the effects of *repetition*. Before we take for granted that our thoughts control our activities which in turn affect our individual life let us remember that every one of us is king over his own kingdom and his subjects are his thoughts.

No one taught in such minute details the power of the subconscious mind the way Jesus did. The Church failed across centuries after him, let alone in this advanced era of learning, to decipher his words and parables. Yet two thousand years ago he taught the parable of the Sower and explained it to his followers at their modest level of comprehension: "*When any one hears the word of the kingdom, and understands it not, then comes the wicked one, and catches away that which was sown in his heart. This is he which received seed by the way side. But he that received the seed into stony places, the same is he that hears the word, and anon with joy receives it; yet has he not root in himself, it lacks endurance: for when tribulation or persecution arises because of the word, by and by he is offended. He also that received seed among the thorns is he that hears the word; and the care of this world, and the deceitfulness of riches, choke the word, and he becomes unfruitful. But he that received seed into the good ground is he that hears the word, and understands it; which also bears fruit, and brings forth, some an hundredfold, some sixty, some thirty*". (Mat. 13:19.)

What then is the Master saying here? He is literally teaching the power of the subconscious mind and how to interact with it. Before we translate his words into our modern understanding we must give the right translation to some words from their original Ancient Greek. The "sower" for instance, has been mistranslated from the two Greek words "*Speiro*" and "*Autos*" which actually translate to "*scatter or sow*" and "*of self*" respectively, which introduces us to the true general meaning and its reference to "sowing" the "seeds of thought" into the "self" or more specifically the subconscious mind. Jesus instructed the truth of how sowing the seeds of a desire will begin to germinate and finally appear into our experiential reality.

The "seeds" meant in this context are the "thought forms" sown in the fields of the Subconscious. Jesus explains that some fall in "stony places" and others fall among the "thorns". He is telling us that unless we focus our "seeds/thoughts" instead of allowing them to fall by the wayside they will either fail to sprout or will develop unwanted results among the "thorns". Care should therefore be taken as to where we sow our thoughts, bearing in mind that each one shall generate a corresponding effect in accordance with the Universal Law. "Bad" or negative ones generate the bad while the opposite is true.

The simplistic view Freud and his followers affixed to the subconscious was: "little more than an emotional and impulsive force in a constant tug of war with the more logical and detached conscious mind." This has now shifted to a purposeful, active and independent guide to behavior. Scientists maintain that it is responsible for the vast majority of our day-to-day activities to an extent that we seem mere "zombies" guided by our subconscious. This may seem an exaggeration yet researchers have drawn the line between human consciousness and the subconscious thought process and many psychologists today describe them as an explicit/implicit duo. Both neuroscientists and psychologists have overcome the major barrier to distinguish between conscious and subconscious thought processes. They can be described easily in simple terms: while conscious discharge explicit and declarative thoughts that can be expressed by words, the subconscious emits implicit and controlled ones that are hard to articulate yet they are the impulses that indoctrinate our daily performance.

Examples of how our subconscious implicit desires drive our life into involuntary actions abound in everyday life: A son who hates his father fails in the exams because he subconsciously wants to hurt him. He feels bad having failed but is subconsciously happy having hurt his father. Many children ruin their lives and take to drugs because subconsciously they wanted to take revenge against their parents for one reason or another no matter how illogical it is. Hatred is turned out against people from whom we expected love and against any of our peers who succeed when we don't. We often retort that some people never change. Man's software cannot change when not reprogrammed to dislocate from his unchangeable past. By understanding the working of the subconscious it is possible to drag the present from the past prohibiting the latter's influence on today's actions.

With all its immense wisdom and power the subconscious has one major drawback: It cannot decide on its own. The conscious mind is therefore required to command it and direct it to acquire anything you ask for. All the disappointments in this world result from our ignorance of its powers as well as limitations when actively engaged in our day to day occupations. Before the human evolution started millions of years ago mankind subsisted solely on the subconscious mind; this is how our children today manage to survive as well until age 3. With the development of the brain the conscious mind also developed in humankind the way it starts developing with our children after 3. Before that life undoubtedly went on perfectly: the subconscious was in charge with the same superb qualities of deductive reasoning, intuition, telepathy and ability to connect with the Universal Mind. Yet today our developed conscious mind can network with the subconscious: our soul/mind directly connects with the Universal Mind or God and creates heaven or hell as per our thoughts and desires.

When we read the Scriptures today we wonder how Moses and a crowd of ancient prophets communicated with God on their almost daily requirements. Although Moses and the prophets came up with codes of behavior requiring some sort of analytical brain their subconscious was always the avenue to *talk* to God. This was mostly achieved through spells, trances or dreams that are rare occurrences to us today because of our highly developed analytical minds. The advent of scientific knowledge transferred the major powers of our subconscious to the conscious one thus alienating us from our spiritual roots and creating a rift between us and the sublime Universal Mind Jesus called the Father and asked us to address in our prayer. With today's highly rational and investigative mind people should not wonder why God is not showing up as he used to do to our ancestors; Jesus gave us the answer 2000 years ago: *"Blessed are the pure in heart, for they shall see God."* Today's investigative minds eliminate the purity in the heart and with it the spiritual power of belief: the requisite pathway to God.

Our scientifically educated conscious however is a two-edged sword that can penetrate the layers of our inner mind and coach it to perform miracles. This positively receptive machine however shall only communicate to the sublime Universal Mind our positive messages carrying our desires for development and wellbeing. It also records our negative messages that are not only mirrored back in the like but serve to block the pathways to the Universal Mind. When you place your undivided attention on a certain phobia it can become a reality. A simple example is when you fear that you won't have enough money to pay your bills. If you concentrate on this fear it will surely materialize: you won't be able to pay those bills! The opposite is true. Let me repeat here: Your subconscious does not care if the situation causes you pain; it only gives you what you picture in your mind. Hence the importance of thinking and talking positive and adopt positivism as a way of life. This is how the Law of Abundance works: the energy to create whatever you desire is always there if positively exploited.

You certainly remember the story where Jesus fed the multitudes? He did not manifest food out of thin air but *did multiply* the five loaves and two fishes into tens of thousands through his unshakable spiritual power. Skeptics' arguments about this miracle could go on forever. The real issue behind it is that Jesus wanted to convey a message: there is more than enough of what we need if we will imagine, believe and then engage in the physical activity to bring it about. So rather than saying: "I will not have enough", let us repeat out loud: "There will always be more than enough". Soon you will not only believe in abundance, you will know it is so.

Our trainable domestic pet though protects itself as we have seen from change with emotional—not analytical—responses. Good or bad habits start building at childhood immediately after 3, many of them last for the lifespan. Habit forming starts with a mere suggestion or impression and unless altered, keeps snowballing as more information and practices are added to those already stored until the habit becomes a solid base for day to day initiation. Example: once you learned to drive a car you don't think consciously about it anymore. Allow me to repeat that we always drive subconsciously: many a time we are engrossed with various thoughts during a trip only to wake up and find ourselves parking at our various destinations. Sometimes I am *awakened* while driving and *warned* of a possible danger. I know I am not unique in this routine; many friends and certainly many readers share me this *absent-minded driving*. Certainly the subconscious in this example is comparable to the autopilot in the airplane; it plays such an eminent role in many endeavors we attempt through this life, guiding, coaching and protecting. This is one instance of how the subconscious stores up relations of *learned behavior*. Typing on your keyboard without looking is another of many examples we find in our everyday life.

This immense storage room houses everything that is currently not in your *conscious mind*; the intensity of the imprints in this software depends of the intensity of *feelings* you had imparted at their first encounter. Most of the times, it is not only the memory stored of the incident but also any feelings that went with it at the time it was stored.

Perhaps the most impressive subconscious exertion appears at the human inter-personal level. It influences the interactions among persons. Dr. Forest Shaklee, a noted researcher in this field puts it right: "To gain happiness you must learn to enjoy that which you have. It is not how much you have. It is what we *think* about that which we have that produces happiness. In building a happy, contented life, you must give happiness to others. No one living unto himself will ever be contented with his lot. Your happiness is reflected upon you through the service you give to others. And the thought you give to the creation of happiness will attract a happiness-service from others. Start creating the happiness-habit by producing happy, love-filled thoughts. Happiness is an attribute of love; therefore you can never be happy until you give your love to others."

-11-

The Healing Catalyst

"It is done unto you as you believe."

Jesus

T he implicit assumptions nowadays open to theological debates about Jesus' healing miracles may go endlessly. One truth is prevalent though: they did happen and the testimonials of many including that of the born-blind vouch for them irrevocably. A modern understanding of the *metaphysical Christianity* is now in progress as a *divine science* attempting to reinstate the healing ministry of Jesus and interpret its many aspects in a *scientific* manner. This Spiritual Science that constantly opposed any "materia medica" as a way of realizing wholeness has now achieved a reconciliation of sorts with the medical science, enlarged understanding and established compatibility with the holistic science.

Within the Christian belief cures are accomplished today in the original way practiced much earlier by the first disciples through prayers channeled across the human inner mind and connected with Christ. Jesus wants people to become whole to be able to accomplish even "greater things than his" (John 14: 12). He not only refers—as some modern healers do—to a "cosmic energy" they feel pouring through themselves but also refers to the belief in the possibility of becoming healthy ultimately by God through his visible person. In his times cures were often "signs" or actions that stood for something larger and more fundamental. During the cure of the person born blind on the Sabbath Jesus declared that it is not a question of sin "but (a matter of nature) the works of God becoming apparent" (John 5:6). Today many practices and para-psychological researches support the scriptural connotations that Jesus could actually influence natural forces. This was apparent in his stilling the raged sea. It is just important for us to contemplate this phenomenon for our contemporary assessment of the human nature when a holistic, integrated or Christian cure is considered.

Jesus constantly lived in "positive awe of God" and compassion to people. In normal people nearly all emotions are initially mixed with subconscious stimulations and response mechanisms that vary in strength from one person to another yet with similar patterns. A long process to learn and a complex mechanism to discover by looking at one's own reactions with a view to control instead of suppress. Working on the complex problems abruptly may not be as effective as searching first for related occurrences; the subconscious needs time to assimilate and comprehend the task ahead before going into execution. The *emotional element of belief* would be the basic criteria in this process. Hence our differentiation between "positive thinking" and "positive affirmations" (guiding principles); if this is practiced in a non-egoistic way (the beam in one's eye versus the splinter in the other's eye) without technical manipulations, it might indeed transform the thoughts into a state closer to the divine path.

It is said that many healers (including medical doctors) become ill through healing because they are attached to that which they do especially when they truly feel their intentions of a loving service to another. The plausible reason is based on the Universal Law that any condition or circumstance your soul needs in order to purge something from within yourself, you get. How do you get it is a matter of harmonic convergence between demand and supply no matter what the circumstances of such healing events are; the means is not important. On the other hand a spiritual healer deploys an amount of his positive power equal to the extent needed for healing thus exhausting his positive energy. Jesus said to his disciples when the sick lady touched his garment and got healed: "I felt a *Power* (electrical charge) getting out of me". He truly lost part of his cumulative power and *perceived* it instantly. His major miracles and enlightening speeches were always performed when he *came down from the mountain*.

Up in the mountain Jesus practiced intense concentration in the company the Father dwelling within him. In fact that was the message and example he gave us as God also dwells within us. He would regain up there his greatly refined state of awareness that requires a calm, laser-like concentration to perceive and enter into pure super-consciousness, thus dominating his own as well as others' ordinary conscious states. He would be in full awareness of the higher negative energy crippling the human mind in the form of tension, emotions and restless thoughts: *"come unto me, all you that labor and are heavy laden (with negative loads), and I will give you rest. Take my yoke upon you and learn from me; for I am meek and lowly of heart (positive), and you shall find rest unto your souls."* (Mat. 11:28.) He would bridge from body awareness to pure Spirit consciousness to receive the cosmic subtle energy supported by deep breathing, intense feeling and will power. His human body would rearm again with that energy spread along pathways of muscles, cells, and tissues, preparing the body for the flood-like force of positive cosmic power.

The subconscious is readily amenable to the healing process when the healer, either the self or the medium, allows and facilitates Love. Love is a power that heals yet not the full power; it has to be supported by its other twin: faith. While love is the ability to heal, faith is the command which allows love to deploy its potential. Ideally the healer's role is to provide a clear, surrendered, unconditionally-loving conduit through which God's love can flow. The role of the subject is to provide faith in the power of God's love (the Universal Love as advocated by Jesus) to yield and transform : healing is in fact a transformation. The healer's faith does not negate the necessity of the client's faith but complements it. The process and relationship is co-creative. If these two aspects of the Law of Healing are not present, transformation does not occur. Whenever faith is not consciously acknowledged by the healer, the curative process can still be achieved: faith could be unknowingly present and strong enough in the subconscious mind to generate the makeover.

The Law of Healing, as the Law of Attraction, is the miraculous power that preoccupied human beings since the dim recesses of the past. An inscription was found in an ancient temple that reads: "The doctor dresses the wound and God heals the patient." It is the healing presence of God residing in our subconscious mind. Doctors and psychiatrists don't heal anyone. A surgeon removes the tumor or the block thereby making way for the healing power of God to cure and restore. A psychiatrist attempts to remove the mental block and encourages the patient to adopt a new positive attitude towards harmony, health and peace to flow through your subconscious mind cleansing negative patterns that may have lodged there. This is the infinite healing presence of life which Jesus attributes to Father and the healing instrument of all mental or physical diseases. Anyone of us has had hundreds of healings since we were children. We can all remember how it brought curative results to cuts, burns, bruises, contusions, sprains, etc., and, in all probability we did not aid the healing in any way by the application of external remedies.

Jesus was the Master and pioneer of this Spiritual Science. He taught us healing by faith or what we call today the holistic healing. He was the divine medium who unblocked nature's regular means of access allowing the natural patterns to retake their course. Cleansing the subconscious mind (forgiving sins in his simplified expression) was his first step to prompt this internal machine into action. The second step was the element of belief fortified by removing all negative pulsations from the sick to activate the human healing power: *Your faith has helped you; go and sin henceforth no more.* Jesus empowered his immediate followers to practice this holistic healing: the healing of the body through the cleansing of the soul where the person recognizes his sins, repents, clears them and upkeep his subconscious in a constant positive state. Those followers had no dogmas, ceremonies, rites or traditions. They fulfilled what Jesus the Son of Man taught them directly. They lived as Jesus in their community implementing his teachings step by step and became willingly his followers.

When negative thoughts and events (sins) block that continuous process of regeneration, or misdirect it, the body gets all the repercussions. Hence Jesus' holistic healing addresses that part of the mind where some "disconnect" has occurred to release it so that the healing and regeneration process can continue as nature generally intended it. In fact the healing process consists of calling forth the ability of the subconscious to "re-program" itself on operating the body. Jesus' healing process and the way he taught us to apply our own curing is that we don't have to study our body's anatomy or have a clear idea of how the organs, glands, and various other systems operate; Jesus, his disciples as well as we need not go to such details, the omnipotent healing power was and still is the direct intermediary through our subconscious passage where the Holy Spirit resides.

Jesus' base rule: "do to others as you would have them do to you," should rather be read differently: Do not do to others what you do not want to have done to you, or: A person will reap what he sows; here is where the Law of Attraction reigns supreme. Today's science speaks of action and reaction and that no energy is lost and what we emit are energies that return to the sender irrespective of its positive or negative aspect. Anything we emit has substance or pictures that are always shaped by our desires. They all return to find their programmed space in our subconscious as well as the cells and cellular tissues of our body including our nervous system which contributes decisively to illness or health. Hence the harmony of the body is in relaxing the nervous system, balancing the body fluids and positively programming the subconscious. This is what activates the holistic healing, the purification of the soul and the constant remedial of the body. Disharmony leads to tension in the nervous system, the cells and cellular tissues, the blood stream, the glands and hormones and the body fluids thus leading to dysfunctions in various parts of the organism.

Self healing through the subconscious may seem a joke to many unbelievers and available to the few who have faith and who manage to interact positively with their inner mind. People laughed at Jesus when he told them the girl was sleeping yet when he revived her and order them to give her to eat they bowed before him and glorified God. A procedure has to be followed though that will stop instantly the production of all mental poisons either in you or in the person for whom you are praying for. Jesus asked everybody to leave the girl's house and kept with him only his three disciples and her parents (the believers.) Why? Because propagated negative feelings would not provide proper conditions for the miracle. A precedent to this is what happened to the Master in his hometown Nazareth.

The first step in healing is not to be afraid of the apparent condition at the first encounter no matter how acute or seemingly impossible. The subconscious can heal a cut in your hand in the same facility it would an ulcer in your stomach. The bruise will heal because *you believe* it would as opposed to the ulcer that you don't believe it would. The second step is to realize that the condition is only the product of past thinking or happening which will have no more power to continue its existence. The third step is to exalt mentally the miraculous healing power of God within you and direct your subconscious to take charge and execute. Throughout the process and until fulfillment, live in the *embodiment of your want* with your thoughts and feelings focused on your goal and considering it a *fait accompli that only needs time.* Do not be swayed by human opinion and worldly fears but live emotionally in the belief that it is God's irreversible action taking its course in your subconscious mind.

When we discover our inner powers coupled with the Law of Attraction we have to be careful: we are nowadays in possession of a two-edge sword that can actively work for our bliss or doom. When something bad happens like an illness you may say to yourself "How can this be? I haven't been sitting here asking to get this disease." But it doesn't work that way when your carnal mind is the thinking mind that commands your life. It is that part of you who when you hear of an influenza outbreak starts questioning: "Do I get this?" Or insinuating: "I am getting old." Or: "I am losing memory." When you indulge in such negativities you're forming pictures and feelings in your mind that are seeping to the subconscious. And if there is enough feeling behind them they will be pushed to dominate your daily life in a negative way. In time they may manifest as diseases, illnesses, degeneration and mental disorder; however once you learn how *not* to accept all the negative things that you have told yourself or what others have said about you the process will be automatically reversed.

Emotions that surge through you and trickle into your subconscious cause physical reactions somewhere in the body. A minor upset may take a couple of days to register as a headache or backache; a more vehement explosion of anger or hatred directed at someone could result in an acute case of ulcers or colitis because that emotion keeps pounding your body. Let us repeat here that as negative emotions have their negative effects so too do positive emotions with their positive effects. We now know from various scientific researches that people who are involved in loving marriages and relationships live longer than people who live alone because of the mental and physical support they share. Joy and peace which spring from love help the nervous system function at an optimum level. Love comes first and foremost; when you put your hand on your friends and loved ones allow this hand to be a vessel of love. When you hold hands with someone think love, God's love, not love when . . . or love but . . . or love if . . . just love. This is the pure, unconditional and universal love Jesus proposed as the prime requisite for the Kingdom of God.

A common occurrence in our everyday life is the fear-based pain. People unconsciously fear pain because they do not understand nor accept that pain is actually an act of healing.

All experienced pains are those which are leaving the body and not introduced into it. There is no pain ever being introduced into the body. When people endure pain they experience situations and circumstances drawn by the soul for the purpose of realizing the separation from the self. In other words pain is one way people experience this separation. It is an important part of the healing process that ensures our growth: we feel pain to get our teeth, to keep them and to lose them; yet pain is perceived as enemy because people seek comfort more than growth: they rush to doctors or pharmacies for pain killer poisoning their systems with chemicals. In enduring pain and suffering lies yet an infinite wisdom: this is the drastic measure to elicit the surrender of the separate tyrannical ego in the human personality and yield to the supreme power and majesty of God. From this state of transcendence *true humility is born* and a true healer can attain unconditional love through his absolute self. Pain is a purifier of the self, a challenger to man's endurance and a transformer of his personality. It is the "Narrow Door" Jesus advocated that leads to harmony and happiness.

-12-

The Pioneer

*"I will give you what no eye has seen, what no
ear has heard, what no hand has touched, what
has not arisen in the human heart."*

Jesus

For his colorful parables Jesus drew imagery from
observation of the socio-cultural scenes to pierce the
subconscious minds. He was aware of the human
subconscious powers throughout his meditations and its
archetypal imagery at the deepest level of collective human
memory where he drew his images and symbols inherent to the

Kingdom of God: sowing and reaping, forgiveness, humility, preparedness etc; and in major parables he offered a full working description of the subconscious mind. His related explanations and conclusions reiterate spiritual considerations and offer practical applications to stimulate a meditative or contemplative prayer.

We contend throughout this study to develop perception and a sense of identity with the indwelling Christ to serve as a helpful petition manual for readers whose comprehension accommodates a modern type of contemplative spirituality. It is not limited to those who appreciate or at least tolerate this spiritual turn-around; hence the repetitive references to reputable works of modern historical and literary biblical scholarship. These resources may not be convincingly integrated with the established psychological premises, although psychological considerations dominate our interpretations of the parables which show little harmony with the typical findings of many contemporary clerics.

Jesus came to Earth to teach humanity how to live a happy, healthy and abundant life and show human beings who they really are, what their true destiny is and how to realize it. Certainly events and circumstances took another course after his Ascension and the true meaning of these teachings was largely lost for two thousand years. The obvious reason is that the gospels were written with many codes, metaphors and overstatements inherent to the mind and language of the old Middle East that only those who are ready to understand them could do so. Many who seized these great works had at that time—as well as now, no clear idea of the true meaning; hence our endeavor today to reinterpret the many valuable lessons that are of great significance to everyone.

The subconscious was Omni-present throughout the parables although some of them were solely devoted to explain its characteristics and the way to understand them by "whoever has ears to listen . . ." Here is one: *"So is the kingdom of God, as if a man should cast seed into the ground; and should sleep, and rise night and day, and the seed should spring and grow up, **he knows not how,** for the earth brings forth fruit of herself; first the blade, then the ear, after that the full corn in the ear; but when the fruit is brought forth, immediately he puts in the sickle, because the harvest is come."* (Mar. 4:26.)

Undoubtedly the power of the subconscious mind is specifically and explicitly illustrated in this parable. Any modern psychology professor would not be able to invent a better parable to describe it. The Thought Forms *germinate* and grow until they can eventually manifest as palpable objects after which they can be harvested and experienced. The "ground" is a metaphor for the *field* of the Subconscious where the seeds/thoughts are sown either consciously or unconsciously. Jesus' saying: *should sleep, and rise night and day, and the seed should spring and grow up* means that once the *seed* has been sown in that fertile ground that most people are unaware of it will first germinate, then sprout, and finally develop into the vivid experience as a waking certainty.

Yet the most meaningful words are: *he knows not how,* referring to the fact that the subconscious, once programmed to execute a task may resort to ways and means *unknown to the person*. These fully developed Thought Forms mature into fruition while people *have no idea* where they came from. They often ascribe them to superstitious guesswork such as *luck* or *misfortune* depending on the *good*, fruitful seed or the *bad* ones that produce weeds. The fertile ground of the Subconscious never judges nor distinguishes as we have seen the good seed from the bad but accepts any sown seeds regardless of their characteristics.

Jesus' concludes: *But when the fruit is brought forth, immediately he puts in the sickle, because the harvest is come.* Here the Though Forms have matured; the task is complete and harvest can be made available with joy. This is the natural outcome of the physical Universe of matter and it is now experienced and enjoyed. You have read earlier in this book that we are closest to access our Subconscious in those twilight minutes before and after sleep when we are in a trance state and where our brainwaves weaken down and away from observing and interacting with the routine physical things. This is what Jesus confirms: "And *should sleep, and rise night and day*, and the seed should spring and grow up."

The main point behind this parable is that we still skim only the surface of the unfathomable depths and powers of the subconscious that Jesus elucidated two millenniums ago. It teaches the great truth about the existence of those fertile fields in the Inner Mind. Thought Forms can be sown there either consciously in accordance with our needs or unconsciously by simply reacting to events around us. Our Subconscious toils relentlessly in attending to our needs either influencing the body in the case of healing or the Universal Mind in case of external wishes, bringing them to full fruition where the harvest may be carried out.

Jesus' parables have different messages to humans at their various times and cultures. They are applicable to his era and existing level of comprehension as well as to ours. Hence his words: "Heaven and Earth may vanish but a word of my utterance would not." Those stories still bring to mind vivid pictures carrying concentrated messages about life applicable to all ages, societies and intelligence, most certainly ours. Example: one of the principles of hypnosis in dealing with the subconscious is, as we discussed earlier, the intense repetition to convince this internal machine of our final and intense desire. It is depicted in two of Jesus' parables: The Midnight Friend and the Unjust Judge that clearly address this issue. In the first (Luk.11:5), Jesus tells of a man who knocks at his neighbor's door at midnight and requests some food for a friend who has arrived at his house unexpectedly. At first the friend said, "Do not bother me." but because the man was *persistent* the friend got up and gave him as much food as he needs. Likewise the subconscious, our friend next door, is resistant to change but through *persistence* it will grant what is requested. Jesus concludes by saying: *"Ask and it shall be given to you, seek and you shall find; knock and it will be opened to you. For everyone who asks receives; and he who seeks, finds; and to him who knocks, it shall be opened."*

The same issue is treated in "the Unjust Judge" (Luk.18:1), who does not fear God and respects no one. A widow keeps coming before him for unwarranted protection from her opponent. As the woman *persists* the judge yielded and said, "Because she bothers me I will give her legal protection. Just by continually coming, she wears me out." This parable hardly needs any interpretation; one comment is due though: the human subconscious is a brute, merciless and insensitive machine exactly like the inequitable judge, hence Jesus' picking the correct resemblance.

Sowing the thought/seed in the subconscious was further portrayed by the Master in his *mustard seed* parable: *"Another parable he put forth unto them, saying: The kingdom of heaven is like a grain of mustard seed, which a man took, and which indeed is the least of all seeds: but when it is grown, it is the greatest among herbs, and becomes a tree, so that the birds of the air come and lodge in the branches thereof"*. (Mat.13:31.)

Before we rationalize this parable perhaps we should quote a statement by Carl Jung assessing in modern terms the Law of Growth in the subconscious. He said: **"The great principle since the beginning is that Heaven is infused into the Man, the Microcosm who reflects the star-like nature and thus, *the smallest part and end of the work of creation contains the*** *whole."* Jung means that every single human being has a "Star" nature. Da Vinci depicted this star showing a man standing upright extending his arms horizontal to his body and placing his feet as far apart as possible, thus fitting exactly into a 5 point Star. This is true no matter what any man's individual build.

Back to the Master's parable we perceive that everything in creation originates as a *seed* beginning with the Source, God; and when it sprouts it begins to grow from something as tiny as a mustard seed—note the first embryonic human cell—before branching out in all directions into a mighty tree so large that birds can shelter in its branches. Irrespective of its growth the tree always reflects its origins—the tiny seed. The mustard tree with its Latin name "Salvadora Persica" was very common in Palestine in the times of Jesus who picked it as the best discernable example of the miniature that produces the massive.

In this teaching the seed is emblematic to the dormant faculties of life and intelligence which can sprout and eventually come to fulfillment. The mustard seed is reminiscent that everything in creation irrespective of its growth is a perfect reflection of its origin. This same tiny seed was once used by the Master to underline the importance of faith no matter how scanty: "If you have Faith as a grain of mustard seed". This Law of Growth exemplified by this seed is a further indication of planting a Thought Form in the Subconscious garden that, when nourished with faith will sprout and grow until it manifests as the fruit of the thought upon the plane of vibration from where the thought originated.

The more we rationalize the parables, the more we find stories about everyday life which have parallels in the psychological and spiritual life of every person that attest to the fundamental stature of Jesus the metaphysician and psychologist, where healings and other miracles come as a byproduct of such stature. Their hidden, metaphysical meaning once disclosed would offer a better understanding of his powerful and practical teaching. It is an esoteric knowledge applicable to anybody's life when one is bent on reaping the spiritual and material rewards associated with it. The more we decipher their concealed significance the more we dwell in Jesus' Kingdom of God in its plain simplicity: our positive human mind.

Let us now enter this Kingdom of the Mind and read the parable of the Sower: "*A sower went forth to sow; and when he sowed, some seeds fell by the wayside, and the fowls came and devoured them up; some fell on stony places, where they had not much earth; and forthwith they sprang up, because they have no deepness of earth; and when the sun was up they were scorched; and because they had no roots, they withered away. And some fell among thorns; and the thorns sprung up and chocked them. But other fell into good ground, and brought fourth the fruit, some a hundredfold, some sixtyfold, some thirtyfold. Who has ears to hear, let him hear.*"(Mat.13.3.)

Jesus is explaining to us here the different levels of perceptions: The subconscious is the soil where our spiritual seeds or Thought Forms are sown. It provides different grounds for perception depending on how careful—or careless the sower is. Implanting our thoughts should always target the deep, fertile soil of our mind with resolve and emotional determination to produce their boundless harvest; careless throwing of our concepts falling on the peripheral sideways will either short-live or choke amid our various negativities.

In another parable, *the leaven*, he refers to the positive implementation that would free the mind from its negativity and create a wholesome material for creativity: "*The Kingdom of God is like unto leaven, which a woman took, and hid in three measures of meal, till the whole was leavened.*" (Mar. 3.33.) Even a tiny measure of positivity would promulgate a heavenly state of mind that will grow and absorb us.

It is also exemplified in *"the dragnet that was cast into the sea, and gathered of every kind; which, when it was full, they drew to shore and sat down, and gathered the good into vessels and cast the bad away. So shall it be at the end of the world; the angels shall come forth and sever the wicked from among the just . . ."* (Mat.13.47;) similarly the subconscious net gathers any good or bad things that sift into it. Our work at the shore of life is to maintain and use our angelic (positive) state of mind by casting the negative thought into the fire. The *angels* allude to God's positive messages that enrich our pure spirit and pursue it to produce that *born-again* status in our subconscious; this second birth in one's spiritual life is that same *renaissance* Jesus vainly attempted to explain to Nicodemus. The end of the world means the end of our personal material life where, minutes before expiry, the human being reviews his life record of good and bad deeds: the final and decisive programming of his subconscious that determines his phasing in to *Heaven* or *Hell*.

The parables were Jesus' best attempt to stir his audience and unlock their fastened consciousness into an open awareness. It is a hypnotic overture in human communication directed to the subconscious to bring about the desired thought or action. This compares to a human adult or better still, children being told a story: their eyes are wide; they are completely absorbed; in a word, *they are in a trance.* There is something for the conscious mind to be occupied with while the real meaning of the story gets directly into the subconscious. In fact the parables were far more powerful than simply explaining the point; a story allows the subconscious to learn on its own. Let alone that the issues the Master promulgated were beyond the limited intelligence among his listeners; those among them that targeted the subconscious characterization were certainly filed for our sophisticated era of advanced knowledge certainly to reactivate our dwindled faith.

-13-

The Contamination

*"Men are built, not born . . . . Give me the
baby and I'll make it climb and use its hands
in constructing buildings or I'll make it a thief.
The possibilities of shaping in any direction are
almost endless . . ."*

John Watson

The human subconscious as well as the animal instinct
is born in the same instance the first cell is formed
in the womb. In the animal world it continues to be
a limited instinct with a meager degree of development while

in the human the evolved conscious mind is gradually added throughout the baby's advancement into awareness where it starts to feed and indoctrinate the unlimited subconscious.

The human subconscious houses information from both inherent and inherited knowledge; inherent knowledge is from our species and depending of your rank as naturalist or spiritualist you may call it the human instinct or the *soul of God*: our appellation throughout this book. In the former it is much like the salmon who knows to swim upstream to spawn: in the latter it is the human-held knowledge of this God-created species. Inherent knowledge differs from the inherited as to its source; it operates along the bloodlines. Talents and abilities possessed without prior learning are many times the result of our inherent knowledge while habits, mental and spiritual developments are our cumulative inherited experiences and impressions.

As the inherent, cumulative data was to a great extent implanted in our subconscious while we were mere fetus in our mother's womb, here comes the tremendous impact of the mother's behavioral attitude towards her unborn baby that most mothers don't seem to realize. They cannot be blamed for their ignorance; what they are reading in the following pages though is perhaps the shocking revelation for each one of them as well as to all parents.

The moment the seed implants itself in the womb and only within three days from the formation of the first cell the thoughts of the mother begin to encroach its space to decide whether the child that will be delivered in nine months is going to be an ordinary sinful mortal or a dedicated son of God! Such are her huge responsibilities every hour of these nine critical months not only in eating the right food and doing the right exercises but most importantly in thinking positive and being in the company of loving and cheerful people. With such a strong mental makeup this child will definitely not be an ordinary mortal!

The conception event is not merely a biochemical process but an emulsion of the parents' persona, thought processes and belief systems many of them affected earlier by wrong programming. Such values are encoded in the DNA of the first cell. Within the next three days the mother's thinking or behavior are not important as the fetus leads its own life under the guidance of the divine remote control that we call the subconscious. The mother uses the blood as a carrier to pass along nutrients, oxygen and hormones to the developing fetus on the one hand and with her *emotions and belief systems* on the other, whereby one set of nutrients builds the body while another set builds the child's subconscious. The basic fetus' subconscious is pure and unpolluted; the influence it receives from the mother whether positive or negative determines its future shape. When she thinks lovingly, optimistically and cheerfully such emotions are imprinted in the tender layers of her baby's subconscious. The opposite is true: she is her child's only contact with the outside world.

Such is the important task on the pregnant woman: the nucleus formation of her child's future personality. When the mother firmly believes in godly qualities in her child such beliefs are induced in his now rapidly evolving psyche. Her continuous and consistent dwelling in these ideals creates an aura around herself attracting the divine, angelic forces of the cosmos. Such forces are directly attracted towards her womb as well as to her human entourage. And when the child is born it won't be a surprise to her in seeing people at her doorstep adoring the newborn!

That is exactly what happened to the Virgin Mary. She is deservedly cherished, sought and worshipped all over the world. True, unlike other mothers she was conceived by the Holy Spirit. She was elated to be "the handmaid of God" and "the blessed one among women." She released her song glorifying Him. Certainly her unshakable belief that she was carrying the long-awaited Messiah made her inject powerful godly emotions into her fetus let alone birthing, nursing and rearing him as the *chosen one of God*. Mary instilled subconsciously much of who Jesus was into him just as mothers everywhere may instill values into their children. She was willing to be the servant of God even though she did not expect what it was going to entail. No mother rears a child keenly wondering if he will be killed in his thirties. Mary is a flagrant example to be followed by all mothers at all times.

Programming our inner mind begins therefore in the womb. When a child is born, no wonder that only positive and powerful thoughts should continue to be the formative process throughout the first critical years. This foundation is the sole determinant of how a child is going to turn out later in life. The mother's thoughts continue after birth to shape the subconscious of the child whether it is immunity towards biological diseases or the right approach to handle life's complexities.

A child until the age of 5 years is constantly in the first round brainwave state, extremely impressionable and open to learning. This is a natural cosmic provision of the Universe due to the fact that a child needs to establish him or herself in the physical world as soon as possible through his survival struggle and preparation for the upcoming life experience.

A child, like the subconscious Mind will never question what he or she is told by their parents, relations, school teachers and other authority figures; they simply accepts everything on trust as fact. Thus a child is *programmed* and is generally running on that program for the rest of his physical life unless such a program is *updated* at a later stage. Often the child grows up as a version or even a "clone" of his parents and grandparents as Jesus said: *"Fathers' failings are traced in the sons to the third and fourth generation."* This is why whole generations in many societies live the same sort of life in almost every respect: to them it is quite *normal.*

Thus all the information that has been stored in our subconscious since our conceptual months and later childhood form our *belief systems* which influence how we act as individuals and the things we believe in. Information that enters the subconscious varies in its intensity according to the age cycles of our life. Certainly our first 6 years of life will have the greatest inpact on shaping our subconscious mind. This is because when we are born we must learn how to react to the happenings of our new environment and the way the world works around us. Therefore the first people to have an influence on our mind are our mothers, parents and relatives.

Children are natural believers and they have very good imagination skills. To them, anything is possible until *an adult convinces them otherwise.* Jesus knew that lack of belief clogs up the energy flow between the conscious the subconscious, hence his assertion: *"You must be as little children to enter the Kingdom of God".* We must use our creative mind as children and believe that what we desire *will become a reality*; whatever was visualized in our imagination will enter the physical and take for granted that whatever we want to happen has already happened. This is how we send a complete picture of the event to our subconscious for the creation process to begin.

Two millenniums ago Jesus knew and taught that children work very hard at trying to understand their surroundings. With their immature brains and limited experience they are great observers but horrible interpreters. As adult role models we have to be aware of what images and concepts we are conveying to the children around us. Mistaken ideas programmed in a child's subconscious become *his engraved certainties.* Jesus was adamant in addressing this disastrous, criminal programming: *"But whoso shall offend (negatively indoctrinate) these little ones which believe in me (have the same child/mind of God,) it were better for him that a millstone were hanged about his neck, and that he were drowned in the depth of the sea."* (Mat. 18:6.)

Jesus could not be more ruthless with the children's negative indoctrinators. He realized they are constantly observing, interpreting and storing information into their amenable subconscious. These billions of thoughts and experiences become later the truths which *run and direct* his or her life. The challenge is to help a child to interpret what s/he sees and hears in ways that can be used later as proof that s/he is capable, loveable and responsible.

Throughout the ages and still today a devastating contamination process takes its course where scores of mistaken beliefs and misconceptions have been stored in the subconscious minds of youngsters who constantly make poor decisions later; involve themselves in self destructive behaviors such as drugs or turning away from learning.

It is a terrible thing to *offend* any of the little ones and there is a deep sorrow or *woe* put upon the world because of these types of offenses. As a general rule the offender is usually a victim himself; either he was abused as a baby or offended as an adolescent. The offender exhibits rigid, religious, legalistic and high morals: s/he may not realize the tremendous effects taking such innate behavior as normal.

Perhaps the verb offend does not deliver the true meaning of Jesus' Aramaic word *Assara* which means mislead or delude. Delusions will always be unavoidable and to whoever the man or woman that brings them against these little ones there will be a deep sorrow or *woe* put upon them. Jesus strictly cautions people to despise the little ones that *believe upon him*, meaning those who have the same pure mind he has because they still hold their angelic characters and the face of the Father is always looking toward them.

Jesus is conveying another implication here: the men and women who believe in him and experience that "renaissance" conversion in their subconscious have become pure as little children. Once people pass from darkness into light they now possess the mind of Christ similar to an innocent, humble little child. Except men and women become as little children and remain this way they will not access the Kingdom of Heaven. Doors are wide open for them to experience a conversion and become as little children; when the trials and temptations come along later they begin to fight their individual battles again, where they may lose this "little child" nature.

After 6 years of age the subconscious now has a foundation of information or a database of sorts to work with. As the years go by a child compares all incoming information against what s/he already has. This means some information may be rejected, modified or added. This tweaking process typically occurs during the teenage years after which it becomes much more rigid and harder to alter. Jesus however taught us how to modify our beliefs in the subconscious after our teenage years and precisely when we reach adulthood and the repeated exposures we have to take over a prolonged period of time in order for the subconscious to be modified again. This is what we will address in the following chapter.

Applied psychology discovered today that the subconscious programming received as a child and its resulting thinking processes that have been established as habits after childhood greatly affect the power of belief. It constitutes a deterrent to the manifestation from occurring because of the negative tape loop that is consistently running in that mind.

Jesus realized and professed throughout his teachings that as time elapses and children begin to experience life their belief systems become limited based on what they are taught by those close ones, initially the family. Although this self limiting programming is instilled by those that most care, in the majority of cases it is done totally with the best intention in mind and only comes about because of what those that pass on these self limiting beliefs were taught and have come to understand to be the truth. Many parents innocently inject in their children seeds of doubts inherited and imprinted in their own minds. Jesus was resolute against this practice which may explain why he told his captured audience when his unbelieving family struggled to see him: *"behold my mother and my brothers! For whosoever shall do the will of God (follow my positive guidelines), the same is my brother, my sister and mother."* (Mar. 3:35.)

Children pick up clues and impressions from the environment on how to behave and what to believe. Families that are in constant battles arguing, squabbling and deploring their luck constitute bad examples to their children. The Church seldom notices this important facet in its catechist teaching. Soon enough children develop a lack of trust and may eventually either leave the Church when they are old enough or attend its services as a mere social habit. Children's self-concepts at this early age constitute a very important part of how they grow, behave, think and most importantly how they think of their religion. Parents and religious educators have to assume that role model and evaluate the important task in front of them which will determine the personal and spiritual life of their children. Whatever self-concept they indoctrinate in their unpolluted subconscious minds will determine the way they perceive their future world.

One of the most endearing traits of children is their innocence added to a natural curiosity. Their first impression when they walk into a room or visit a zoo formulates in their minds endless questions for endless possibilities. They are similar to the early explorers who discovered the new continents and they have indeed a whole world ahead to explore. Throughout their transitional passage into adulthood they are trained on what and what not to ask, what is socially acceptable and what is not. Their negative coaching can carry unintended consequences when their subconscious minds are so contaminated to prevent them from breaking out as they grow older, and if this carries over later in their life, they find themselves swept into the negative mainstream that will limit their abilities and obstruct their creativity. The time then will come for a cleansing process in order to explore the world anew from a different perspective.

The cruel penalty Jesus imposed on the children's negative indoctrinators was always subject to my incredulity before I became aware of the subconscious functioning and most certainly before I became a father. Fatherhood has taught me more about God's child/mind than all my courses in psychology and spirituality combined. Children are not sinless and devoid of sneakiness as every parent can attest. These aspects are inherent thanks to the negative electric current in the human body as well as the innate imprints their subconscious acquired even while in their moms wombs. But no matter how "devilish" their comportment may appear the pure, angelic touch is clearly discernable. Thus when I read passages like (Mat.18-2 & 19-13) or (Mar. 10-15) or (Luk.18-17,) I saw a new light in Jesus' love to children as well as a scientific outlook in his teaching.

One prominent passage is worth considering: *"Jesus said, "Suffer the little children to come unto me, and forbid them not: for of such is the kingdom of God. Verily I say unto you, whosoever shall not receive the kingdom of God as a little child, he shall not enter therein."* (Mar. 10:14.) Jesus was much displeased when he noticed the disciples' rebuke to those who brought the children to him. And when those disciples asked him who is the greatest in the kingdom of heaven? Jesus called a little child to come to him and set the child in the middle of them and explained: anyone who wants to enter into the kingdom of heaven must become converted to return as a little child. Whoever humbles himself or herself as the little child he had set in the midst of them, the same is greatest in the kingdom of heaven. In addition, whoever receives a person humbled as a little child in the name of Jesus receives Jesus also.

The concept of "sin" is the whole issue in the subconscious perception of what is *bad* or *good*. Long, the noted psychologist says: "The subconscious has no discrimination about right and wrong. However it can be programmed by upbringing religion and society to believe deeply in certain concepts." For example, I was raised to believe that table manners were a mark of intelligence and social status. When I came to live in Texas where people ate with their fingers and put their feet on the table in public places I was in a state of shock which has never left me to this day. My friend's daughter believes that to be spiritual she must not wear makeup or fancy clothing, so she goes around unkempt and bedraggled. Nothing logical can shake this conviction of the subconscious. The point is that there is no logic to the rules that the low self lives by. The lessons of childhood may have been misunderstood as a child would not always comprehend his parents' scolding. No amount of middle self logic can overcome this strange programming in the subconscious. Therefore, reprogramming and regular clearing of guilt are essential in the steps toward bringing the selves into unity."

Adulthood opens all doors to the subconscious contamination. For those purified minds that endured the "born-again" tribulation and achieved the positive renewal are subjects day and night to countless negative assaults especially in the wide open worldly society we are integrated to. The single, most defying challenge to any man or women today is how to integrate in the *mainstream* while living a marginal yet clean life as a *black sheep* in this ambient society especially at a time where the whole world has become a tiny global village.

People share everything today most importantly communication and cultural exchange. Jesus warned many times of the "forces of darkness" that invade the yielding, purified minds and gave the solution for such a dilemma.

Do not tell anybody said the Master; while you are still new at creating what you want, keep your thoughts and goals to yourself. It may come as a surprise to you but many people do not want you to be creative. They want those they know and the things they do to be openly predictable and apparent. As your goals come to fruition you will be able to tell others because their negativity cannot penetrate your belief in yourself and in what you are doing. Your spiritual knowledge is your treasure chest. Jesus warned his disciples "not to throw their jewels before the swine lest they trampled them with their feet." The carnal mind is the enemy of the spiritually clean subconscious. It is the *satanic* power integrated to the negative current in our system that yearns all the time to play its destructive role.

-14-

The Cleansing

"Rituals are the outward symbols of the inward desires."

The author

The intimidating thing about the subconscious power is that we have little control over most of its capabilities. As discussed earlier it is energized mainly by two factors: a hybrid of our mothers' minds which we have inherited through both genes and manipulations and the collective experiences, positive or negative, that make up our early life experience. So far very few of us take an active interest in learning how to take control of our subconscious and some of those who know how simply don't take the step. So we go on with our lives letting our past occurrences govern our personalities and control everything we do. As a result of this depressing situation most of the time our subconscious refers to times in our past related to fear and negative experiences. These constitute a hazy pattern that runs our lives. The good news here is that we can reprogram our subconscious to meet our nascent wants and aspirations.

Training your subconscious can be easy and straightforward if you manage to speak the only language it was created to understand: the constructive one. In reprogramming the subconscious through the "born again" process in Jesus' expression, ideals can be injected depending upon previous "programming" and emotions surrounding those ideals whether understood or misunderstood. This delicate method suggests positive ideas which affect the subconscious and stir a positive response; a powerful tool indeed to convince the mind to create a healthy environment outside its electromagnetic shield or inside it. However the "manager of the mind" awaits instructions before getting rid of negative records. Until then it goes on using the same program unless convincingly told otherwise exactly— as e said, like a computer which despite all the hardware cannot run until you enter a program that in turn cannot operate until you touch the keyboard. Entering new human programs is like adding new dimensions to the imagination of the computer and tapping into more of its potential "mind."

Previous natural incarnations in the human mind however are persistent in keeping their imprints. Strong will power supported by belief always meets the receptive subconscious mood that cannot be deceived or tricked. It only yields to the true spiritual ideals and the full natural resonance of the mind that can truthfully penetrate its layers. It is wide open to the positive *truthful* patterns delivered by the conscious; thus the subconscious does not resist the conscious input but rather listens to it patiently before saying "that does or does not agree with my individual programming". When it does not for lack of faith and will power, the complex problems of reconciling the *opposites*, positives and negatives, would emerge causing an *emotional disharmony* and ending up through cheating or disbelief expulsing such disharmonies in the outer conscious life.

Cumulative inputs, millions of them, have penetrated our subconscious since early childhood and dwelt there to become the imprinted C.V. of our personality. Both negative and positive entries have somehow found their way to that hidden niche. All inherited, pre-birth, childhood and adolescence entries have been *posted* in our inner computer. The negative intentional happenings or *sins* have been implanted simultaneously with the positive *ideals* in that vast subconscious field. Jesus was well aware of this swelling buildup; he showed us the best way to cleanse our subconscious in the following parable that was not understood across centuries let alone by many of our churches today: *"the kingdom of heaven is likened unto a man which sowed Good Seed in his field; but while men slept, **his enemy** came and sowed tares among the wheat, and went his way. But when the blade was sprung up, and brought forth fruit, then appeared the tares also. So the servants of the householder came and said unto him, Sir, didn't you sow Good Seed in your field? From whence then has it tares? He said unto them, **an enemy has done this**. The servants said unto him, will you then that we go and gather them up? But he said, nay; lest while you gather up the tares, you root up also the wheat with them. Let both grow together until the harvest: and in the time of harvest I will say to the reapers, gather together FIRST the tares, and bind them in bundles to burn them: but gather the wheat into my barn."* (Mat. 13:24.)

Again, no modern well-versed psychologist can offer a better process for a mature cleansing of the mind. Jesus wanted the human being to let these unwanted negatives implanted in his childhood to grow along with the positives in his subconscious because until s/he grows, one can't distinguish the difference between them. After *growing* it becomes *discernable* to refuse the evil and choose the good as the mind acquires full maturity and willpower. If we weed our garden when we are immature we will pull up the good seed along with the bad. Yet during the time of maturity—*harvest time*—we can remove all the tares that the negative forces—*the enemy* that our carnal mind produces have planted there when we slept (moments of carelessness or lack of control). This is the first step toward renewing our minds and such is the *renaissance* much heralded by the Master.

This mighty tool that Jesus promulgated 2000 years ago has been withheld from us until we spiritually mature. It is that part of our mind which God has kept virgin, reserved to those who will be able to properly handle its powers and capabilities. The brainpower of Christ has changed many things in the past and keeps changing more today. Jesus wanted us to possess and use his brainpower promising us that: *greater things you will be able to do.* He also taught us perseverance as that amazing internal machine *learns by repetition and not by logic.*

That is why you can induce someone to believe in something by *repeating your insinuation instead of using reason.* Injecting new programs in your mind can fix many problems in your personality. Allow me to repeat: Keep this *autopilot* of your life running positively toward enriching this life and not negatively into ruining it. Your repetitive exercise can be termed as an enjoyable art despite all the efforts and hard work. This mind process has to be done every day; we certainly take the effort to go to the gym regularly to be fit; a likewise yet simpler effort should be taken in exercising the mind.

The first step of the process starts with understanding the subconscious patterns and getting aware of them; at this stage you have come to know this mind, befriend it, feel it and listen to what it says. It keeps speaking the whole day and the person can fine-tune his mental ear to listen to what it says and differentiate between the changing positive/negative moods when contradicting thoughts emerge in the mind. Once the person learns through contemplation to pay heed to the subconscious and understands its outlines the time to reprogram has come and the process of elimination is now at hand.

Autosuggestion is a powerful mental training that enables individuals to instruct the subconscious to develop *positive beliefs*. Other methods such as self-hypnosis and constant self affirmations can be used to accomplish this objective. Visualization comes next as popular mind training where an internal mental image is created to effect the behavioral changes. Self hypnosis is another form of intensive visualization essential to consciously attract our wants. Through it we saw images with deep emotions and laser like focus on well defined intents. This is how such thoughts are programmed in our subconscious. Energy's waveforms convert into particles of matter through the power of the subconscious mind. Jesus put this principle in a simple format: *"With what measure you mete, it shall be measured to you; and unto you that hear shall be more given."* Through the Law of Attraction we now know that every action starts with a thought that guides us to deal with life on its own terms. If we think bad thoughts the worse happens to us and with the good thoughts goodness is on its way to us. Our conscious level controls how we discern our surroundings at any given time but is only involved in what we perceive. It takes in what the eyeballs grapple and deposit that information but the process does not end there, for another level is involved in developing mind power: the subconscious.

Cleansing Thoughts open the subconscious to accept positive concepts as reality. This occurrence gradually changes your outer life to match your new inner reality. Cleansing Thoughts are the antidotes to all the negative impulses we've fed ourselves for years. If you've been feeding yourself negative ideas for ten, twenty, or thirty years the positive will certainlyfeel strange for a while. But affirming diligently and assertively the good with Cleansing Thoughts will surprise you of how easy it can be to create the happy and fulfilling life you have always dreamed of.

The *renaissance* development in our subconscious is comparable to a vast field dried by the hot summer sun that it appears barren. When the rains soak the land seeds sprout up with many unwanted weeds the farmer never desired to have. Such weeds did not come with the rains; their seeds were already implanted in the soil itself. This is the case with us: there are subtle impressions in our subconscious that revive themselves when external factors and conditions occur. The cleansing operation consists of gradually emptying all unwanted subconscious inklings and tendencies: the weeds. It may seem an impossible task; but it is not. It is possible to change the contents of mind just as it is possible to sow good seed so as to start replacing the weed. We will experience with great joy that the conscious is storing up the subconscious with arrays of positive impressions. That joy emerges from our controlling and handling both conscious and subconscious minds. Our actions, thinking, and feeling automatically find their way towards this cleansing process: an individual human breakthrough similar to the experience of early explorers' discoveries! Our main obstacle in this exercise is the restlessness of mind and the number of desires that hang around in it. Reducing and managing our desires without creating a vacuum is therefore a must. Discrimination, renunciation, selfless work and devotion are the keys. This is the *psychology of spiritual science.*

Having read so far, away from any distraction or mental evasion, I have no doubt you are now able to access your subconscious mind and dictate your wants and wishes. Yet surfing however through an unclean subconscious is like riding a lumping horse or working with a virus-struck computer: slow, irresponsive and ineffective. In this situation our Thought Forms will not be able to forge that penetrating power to convince our subconscious of our unshakable resolve: the negative viruses we had accumulated in that computer shall not cease to spread doubts prompting our inner machine to tell us: *that doesn't match my programming*; in which case our rejected Thought Forms will hover back over our consciousness.

Reprogramming the subconscious is your powerful mediation to clear out the old, limited beliefs and negative ideas that became deeply rooted patterns and make way to receive the good, positive ones. This process is more possible than you have ever believed. We have by now detailed how the subconscious mind operates and even mentioned cleansing mediations to clear all unwanted beliefs. The time has come to energize and *fill up* new pictures and convictions with higher vibrations and fresh thought patterns to attract effortlessly the higher self image, health, wealth and prosperity on every level.

Let us say it again (*repetition*), we have to envision this vast universe with truly inconceivable dimensions and unimaginable potentialities. *We are part of this immense realm* and our consciousness has access to its virtually infinite depths; despite this enormity that we can dispose of we choose to confine ourselves to meager beliefs and scarce resources that *are not true:* they all have been falsely visualized and trapped in our subconscious to become the traits of our personality.

The time has come to exterminate them. They have been clobbering us long enough in forms of isolations, illnesses, impoverishments and all sorts of daily discomforts. We have the power to overcome such obstacles and change any aspect of our lives through sheer willfulness. What is hazy to us today can through study and strategy be made clear tomorrow. And what is weak in us today can through patience and passion sustenance be made strong in us tomorrow. Our greater self is only a thought away with the esoteric techniques we have acquired. Changing our beliefs has simply become a matter of changing our mind in order to allow the elaborate process of the subconscious cleansing to take its course. By observing our internal dialogue and reversing the content, cadence and certainty of our thoughts in another direction entirely, we can, as an artist before a canvas, repaint a whole new reality before us.

We have also found out that certain acts are performed reflexively or without conscious awareness. For instance, mind goes on thinking bad thoughts despite attempts to control them. From where such thoughts of anger, lust, jealousy, hatred and even desire to harm others, come? Definitely from the negative part of the electrical system that empowers our body triggered by various past downbeat inputs. Same is the case with good or noble thoughts that emerge from our positive part. These two undercurrents (*repetition*) represent our "diabolical" penchant as well as our "angelic" mannerism. Their apparent aspects arise from the subconscious where they became subtle impressions interacting with all our behavioral manners.

Those subtle impressions are now easily remedied through the psychology of spiritual science that will escort you throughout this reading. Emptying the subconscious of all unwanted impressions and tendencies, *the weeds*, is nowadays an easy task for the serious and resolved. It is as possible to change the contents of mind as sowing good garden seeds to start replacing the weed. The moment we decide—a decision is always magnetized our actions, thinking, and feeling should carry purely positive messages that gradually cleanse the subconscious of its dirty contents.

As Jesus taught, cleansing the subconscious must be a serious, mature operation. Rarely any human who attained adulthood would resort to re-injecting negative concepts but is certainly bent on eliminating all the previous ones that crammed his subconscious. This process can be compared to cleaning an old, dirty ink bottle. You cannot have it clean by emptying the ink out so you pour clean water several times shaking it each time until the ink and its remaining residue have been washed out and the bottle contains only clean water. Likewise, it is not possible to drain the mind by emptying the consciousness. What we can do is keep pouring clean spiritual thoughts of positive virtues like love, selflessness, etc . . . until the old, dirty impressions are gradually wiped out. The exercise comes as easy and joyful with our deep intent, exactly as its final reward. This is the *narrow gate* Jesus talked about leading to bliss and beatitude.

The brain cells remember all impressions, experiences and activities of your life; a vast accumulation of unwanted material in the subconscious and the methods to purge them out are now psychologically available. This is also recognized by those who make neurological studies of the brain. To achieve the cleansing process self help techniques are simple and effective in reducing until elimination cumulative subconscious mental garbage or any negative ideological pollutants, thus transforming this mind into a recipient of positive instructions. Before we move to practical applications, it fits to ask ourselves some pertinent questions:

- *Do we feel that our brain has too much information to process? Or unable to express ourselves as clearly as desired? Or in less mental freedom to fly with our imagination or create what we feel we would like?*

- *Does our mind wander away into things unrelated to the circumstances and people around us?*
- *Are our memories disturbing us with unpleasant scenarios?*
- *Are we suffering from new health symptoms?*
- *Do we still have the motivation to enjoy life or are we experiencing times of depression and malaise?*

The number of negative responses determines our need to set aside such negative and obstructing thoughts and explore *the way* to get rid of them. We had indicated that way and we will discuss it again and again. It is called *visualization*, the science by which consciously drawn images and desires are subconsciously produced to become manifested in physical reality. Exercising visualization can best be through either mental contemplation or physical exercise. Let us review both:

Contemplation is the oldest mental drill people practiced and they still do today to achieve a degree of introspection. We repeat again, to get the best results through these methods, an atmosphere of serenity and relaxation conducive to perfect concentration should be available. Away from the rigorous schemes currently known, contemplation should be a relaxing and exhilarating training; this is where you sit, ideally in a quiet and relaxing setting: your dark room, an isolated beach or a secluded spot in nature where no interference would interrupt your visualization. Once there by yourself, dispense with any mundane worry that clubbers your consciousness by a resolute act of will and start interacting with your inner mind.

The noted psychologist Ralph Marston said: *"There is a thought in your mind right now. The longer you hold on to it, the more you dwell upon it, the more life you give to that thought. Give it enough life through repetition and it will become real. So make sure the thought is indeed a great one."* Speaking of repetition, let's repeat that Thought Forms become palpable things. The words we speak or think create our life. Cleansing Thoughts are very powerful means of reprogramming the subconscious. They are most effective when repeated in a quiet and restful state of mind and when the desired outcome is vividly experienced in one's mind and resulting emotions are felt. Morning time is ideal to surround yourself with positivity because your mind is most open and receptive. By using Cleansing Thoughts you will be *tapping into your own unlimited abundance of positive energy.* Your heart and mind will open to the positive changes that are coming your way and so your eyes to the good that's already around you. Used consistently, Cleansing Thoughts will help focus your awareness on your power and ability to manifest your dreams and heal those parts of you that are keeping you *stuck.*

As to the physical exercise, my favorite is what I humbly copied from Jesus when he used *to leave his disciples and climb to the mountain.* Whenever time does not permit, another drill is available in front of the window on my exercising machine. Beside the physical work out that both drills entail, the air intake of rich oxygen, *the Breath of God* that enters the lungs profusely to regenerate both body and soul. Throughout this serene and rigorous discipline away from it all contemplation attains its highest degree of sharpness and visualization becomes laser-sharp: the optimum conditions to access the subconscious.

Breathing is our most basic function and the most essential for survival. Our subconscious tightly controls the automatic breathing rhythm to ensure our continued existence. Yet we yearn for more than survival on this earth and the technique of breathing carries the hidden secrets that give us the mastery of life enabling us to interface with the universe and improve our physical and spiritual levels. The four stages of breathing are: Inhaling, First Pause, Exhaling and Second Pause. Each of these has a specific meaning as they represent the 4 seasons of the year as well as of our life.

For optimum results a breathing exercise can accompany or follow either meditation or physical sport rituals. *Inhale* air through your nose to maximum lungs capacity. This stage brings the outer world and a bit of the universe into your world. It should delight you when you realize that behind the facade and illusion of the world you are now interacting with the Sublime Power that permeates and transcends the mere physical process and enjoying it. In the Bible God breathed life into man, so when man inhales he receives this life force again; the oxygen is the *breath of God*. The *First Pause* is the phase of nourishment and assimilation of the power you have received. With the ingredients that transform the air we transform ourselves. At such moments, silence is born, our atomic composition is changed and we are not the same person we were just seconds earlier. *Exhalation* comes next and only after we absorbed the vital atoms of the air. This phase is similar to giving ourselves to the universe, not to be afraid of it but to enjoy it. The *Second Pause* is different: in the first one you were full of power now you are ready and hungry for another intake that is more gratifying than the first. Your rounds of deep breathing could thus go on for about ten minutes.

During this breathing exercise you become a co-creator in this world and a part of everything. The power of breathing enables you to reconnect with your creator, the universe and the potential that lies within. You get the true feeling that everything is just flowing and changing just like you. You feel *cleansed* and reborn every minute. Jesus undoubtedly practiced this rigorous regimen alone in those secluded mountains. Those seclusions served to re-attune himself with the Father, our Universal God and renew the connection with his divine origin; away from all human mundane trepidations. Within the serene silence that creates openness he would recharge his cosmic battery in preparation for the next round of feats. On each miracle and healing he wrought he would release a burst of this accumulated energy; the incident of the woman with blood issue is a blatant example. We attempt such *feats* daily at a much lower scale with the modest mind power we usually garner and feel by the end of the day the lack of that deployed energy.

New and clean ideas can only fit a liberated mind and new life requisites demand a new consciousness. This is very much in line with the Law of Attraction stipulations. Again, Jesus put it right when he said: *"No man puts a piece of new cloth unto an old garment, for that which is put in to fill it takes from the garment, and the rent is made worse. Neither do men put new wine into old bottles (made then as earthenware not glass); else the bottles break and the wine runs out, and the bottles perish; but they put new wine into new bottles, and both are preserved."* Therefore a clean spiritual consciousness is needed to receive fresh spiritual ideas and knowledge.

This cleansing process is an enterprising scheme that, like any new project, should have its feasibility study before attempting to start it. Are we physically, mentally and above all spiritually geared up to undertake it? And whatever the goal ahead are we aware of the cost involved in order to attain it? Jesus also asserted this preparedness in the following parable: *"For which of you, intending to build a tower, sits not down first, and counts the cost, whether he has sufficient fund to finish it? Lest haply, after he has laid the foundations, and*

is not able to finish it, all that behold it begin to mock him, saying: This man begun to build, and was not able to finish. Or what king, going to make war against another king, sits not down first, and consults whether he will be able with ten thousand to meet that comes against him with twenty thousand? (Luk.14:28.) The latter part of this parable asserts the first: could we with whatever positive forces we can garner meet the seemingly superior negative forces of old ideas and habits, doubts and fears and defeat them? Certainly, if only one more brigade called faith is added to our army we will prevail and emerge victorious.

Positive Thought Forms are constructive. You feel their cleansing flow and you realize that it is not only cleansing your subconscious but it also your whole organism. You feel any negative impulses such as anger, bitterness, feeling of rejection, grief, guilt, abuse and all other downbeat emotions being rinse out of your system giving way to comfort, calmness and peace of mind . . . You pick out more ease with that renewed feelings of relaxation, comfort, serenity and well-being that linger with you even after you come out of this relaxed state.

To sum up and enter the practical sphere with your cleansed subconscious now filled with clear-cut objectives you set out to improve your life and realize your breakthrough, the following regimen (*alertness*) should constitute your daily measures to transform your Cleansing Thoughts into permanent ideals as well as deterrent of any possible relapses:

> **Repetition:** *Make it part of your daily routine. Repeat the affirmation as much as possible.*
> **Emotions:** *Feel what it would be like as if what the affirmation says is already true.*
> **Visualization:** *Create a clear picture in your mind of what it would look like if the affirmation was reality.*

Persistence: *Affirmations take time. Be patient . . . and know the positive results will unfold.*

Belief: *Believe it as all possible: this is the irreversible Law of the Universe that you are now an active part of.*

-15-

The Spiritual Renaissance

"I still have much more to say to you, <u>more than</u>
<u>you can now bear.</u> But when he, the <u>Spirit of the</u>
<u>Truth</u> comes, he will guide you into all truth"

Jesus

Yes. Jesus really suffered the lacking mental capacity of his
disciples let alone his normal audience. He was bent to
explain all the mysteries of the cosmic Kingdom of God
but that was far out of reach of what they could *then* comprehend
even through parable simplifications. Hence he referred them to
the Spirit of the Truth, the more sophisticated mind bestowed

then by the Holy Spirit, the one we possess today, that would further guide them into all truth. That is what happened to Apostle Paul in the past and what is available to us today.

On the other hand the limited ranges of the Aramaic language expressions could hardly carry the dynamic movement of his perception and the far reaching scope of his rationalization. He realized upon his enlightenment that this experience or whatever tribulation he had been through could not be taught because it is alive and personal. It was like describing the beauty of the Aurora Borealis to someone who was blind from birth. Besides, any conveyance may have had an entirely different meaning from one person to the next based on life experience. It is something that must be entered into, embraced and experienced totally with our entire being in relation to our personal experiences. This explains perhaps the reason why Jesus' philosophy is more accessible and elucidated today than in the past. And as in experiencing the work of art we behold a beauty or a truth in ourselves that has been illuminated for us with the help of the artist, likewise this perception in Jesus' message.

The same explanative quandary was obviated in the Master's conversation with Nicodemus. At Jesus' time the Sadducees did not believe in the resurrection of the body. The Pharisees and the Gnostics espoused a vague idea thereof. The Essenes and the early Christians were believers in the actual bodily "resurrection" through the spiritual renewal or the true "spiritual resurrection" that Jesus advocated. These were the *hidden esoteric mysteries* and the *higher secret teachings* which he *shared only with a few.* The public at large in those days as well as in this era of information could not understand the spiritual reincarnation—the subconscious cleansing we know today and the resulting resurrection of being "born again of the Spirit." This is apparent in Jesus' conversation with

Nicodemus the Pharisee doctor who praised the powers of Jesus but *failed to understand* his explanations about such spiritual metamorphosis! It is interesting to review this conversation once more, subject to controversy among church clerics in the past as well as today:

"Jesus replied, "I tell you the solemn truth, unless a person is born again, he cannot see the kingdom of God." Nicodemus said to him, "How can a man be born when he is old? He cannot enter his mother's womb and be born a second time, can he?" Jesus answered, "I tell you the solemn truth, unless a person is born of water and spirit, he cannot enter the kingdom of God. What is born of the flesh is flesh, and what is born of the Spirit is spirit. Do not be amazed that I said to you, 'You must be born again.' The wind blows wherever it wishes, and you hear the sound of it, but do not know where it comes from and where it is going. So it is with everyone who is born of the Spirit." . . ." (John 3:3.)

What Jesus tried to explain to Nicodemus in our modern terms is that *resurrection* of the body is actually a spiritual regeneration of being *born again* following a total subconscious cleansing that in the words of Jesus was *the deliverance of sins* and a total transformation from doctrinal religious thinking toward spirituality; a development to new scientific, metaphysical and religious foundation into universal spirituality. It is the joy and love in knowing that such cleansing *is* that spiritual regeneration and the all-important transition—threshold—which we cross over to resume our real life and real home in *heaven,* the spiritual realm presided by love and its positive links and characteristics. This is the true personality of each *born again* with all the requisites for accessing the Kingdom of God.

Jesus compares the working of God's spirit to that of the wind. The effects of the wind can be seen but the wind itself is not seen or controlled. The wind goes where it wishes and does what it will and so does the spirit. The spirit goes about the life-giving work and no man controls it. No one by his works, striving, or manipulation can direct this spirit; but when the spirit brings about the new birth the effects are evident. We know it is the work of God, unseen and beyond our control, yet it characterizes our new whole personality. Such personality carries an ethereal, glorified body governed and directed by the spirit, the holy spirit of God that moves about like the wind! This total transformation was beyond the grasping of Nicodemus; he left Jesus bewildered by his explanation yet believer enough in his unfathomable powers to become his low profile disciple.

To many Jews being born a Jew was sufficient enough to enter the kingdom of God. They even believed that Gentiles are born *lost*. Even the Jerusalem church leaders had to be forcefully convinced that God had purposed the salvation of Gentiles (Ac.10:11,) and even then the practice of many Jewish believers did not match their conviction. Paul hit hard on this point: "Israelites are not true Israelites, only *those who trust in the atoning work of Jesus Christ are true Israelites, whether their racial origins are Jewish or Gentile*" (Gal. 3:28).

The above mentioned issues take me back to my early spiritual ignorance just like Nicodemus. I wondered how possible for a human being to be born again? When I understood the mind of Jesus I felt the difference and the gradual departure from the previous carnal mind . . . and flesh. I knew to be born again requires an open heart and a liberated mind. I realized that when we are really born again our thoughts, actions and way of life change completely and so our old self.

Nicodemus has not been given Jesus' understanding as well as ours today about the subconscious cleansing. He must have witnessed Jesus at the outset of any miracle saying to the sick: "Your sins are forgiven," thus clearing the subconscious from all negativities and preparing it for action. This stance, *"Just to show you that the Son of Man has a (divine) power to forgive sins"* was in itself a *transitory spiritual renaissance* that the Master wished it to be permanent by referring the healed to his religious chief or ordering him/her: *"Go and sin no more;"* as to his close disciples and devotees who achieved such cleansing he commanded *thorough watchfulness.*

No wonder Nicodemus was puzzled, prompting Jesus to tell him: *"Do not be amazed that I said to you, 'You must be born again."* He was more confused and even speechless when the Master stated that an individual who was "born of the spirit" would actually be a *spirit* or a spiritual essence devoid of all negatives and something extra-physical: a being in the spiritual dimension rather than the physical. Nicodemus was beginning to realize that he was now looking at the fullness of the Spirit world but he could not come to terms with it because he was looking at the Law and Prophets in a carnal mind. He needed to be born again to see into the Spiritual kingdom of God and let go of the shadow of the Law. Nicodemus must have left this conversation in grim mystification: here is a man who thinks he has reserved a prominent residence in heaven and a Teacher telling him that he is not even going to get there as he is. He first must be spiritually born again.

Things did not change much two millenniums later. The majority among Christians today are modern Nicodemus typecasts. There is no doubt that the need for transformed minds has never been greater. There was a time when most of society held a fixed body of opinion to be true. But today we live in a philosophical jungle having many ports of origin from which people attempt their journey to *truth.* However the desired destination for the Christian mind has never changed: the mind of Christ. Personal makeover begins with the acquisition of that mind. Our minds, wherever they wander, are wired in the innate Jesus spirit where many of our thoughts, images, feelings and perceptions subconsciously emanate. Even spontaneous actions are based on cognitive memories deeply rooted in that mind. Paul taught that transformation based on reprogramming the mind when he told the Romans: *"And be not confronted to this world; but be you transformed by the renewing of your mind, that you may prove what is that good, and acceptable, and perfect, will of God."* (Rom. 12:2).

This transformation of the mind cannot be accomplished by accident or reached by simply drifting toward it but a call to choose the life and then live out the design that will renew our minds; a disciplined focus and a change in the way we exercise and train this mind. We have already known that the subconscious can be trained like a domestic pet by means of a strict discipline and resonating repetitions. Paul taught in many of his epistles that we can rid ourselves of anxiety, double-mindedness and a myriad of negatives through good focusing and positive thinking disciplines. Time and perseverance are the essence.

Renewing our mind is definitely not a quick-fix approach but a tenacious determination with no intention for faltering or giving up. Our early gains over the dark forces are our initial working capital. At this stage of early successes in our endeavor Jesus reminds us: *"He who has will be given and added, and he who has not shall be taken from."* As we grow in our commission and the longer we travel on the path of conforming our thinking and ideas this process of mind transformation becomes more automatic and natural. And the more our minds are measured up the more our understanding will gather momentum.

Again, the renaissance (from the French verb "renaitre" or born again) of the subconscious begins with consciously transforming our ideas, images and feelings. This conglomerate of thoughts and feelings packed in our inner computer informs and influences our decision-making and affects our willpower. Our ideas are beliefs based on our life experience and worldview. Our images are concrete and specific pictures or memories of life. Our feelings are the passions and the desires we experience. The mind is the intersection where ideas and images encounter the body which feels and acts. It is here where ideas translate into action. It is where our beliefs are converted into faith. It is at this meeting that the saying "as a man thinks so he is," comes true.

The bondage of the mind begins with conforming its ideas, images, and feelings. These are primary targets to the negative outbursts of our carnal mind. Once that mind is in control of our beings we become in bondage, gripped by our negative strongholds. Unless we stop those negative assaults we drift to the service of a new master usually called Satan, where we feel completely submissive and defeated. Such strongholds have been experienced as arguments or pretensions that position themselves as alternatives to the positive truth. In reality and irrespective of their various posturing, they become effective and well seated in the postmodern mind. From the beginning our negativity's primary strategy was to instill in the mind the basic message conducive to all temptations: *Take charge, take what you need, and take it now.* These are the slogans of the carnal minds that are themed to the pattern of this world; the banner of those whose minds are in bondage.

What did Jesus really mean by *water* in explaining to Nicodemus the rebirth from "water and spirit?" Is it the purifying washing water for either cleansing the body or the baptism water that purifies the soul? Or is it the womb water that contains the fetus? Or rather the water that constitutes 95% of the human body? Surely Jesus considered the two purest elements of nature: water that sustains the body and oxygen that sustains the soul as the main supportive ingredients of the human renaissance. In this context he discouraged his disciples from even eating regular meals and recommended abstention from bread: *"A man lives not by bread alone."* Certainly a person is born from the little pool of the womb's water whereby his spirit starts shaping up as his subconscious is gradually indoctrinated. This is the first birth that exposes the subconscious to endless pollutions necessitating a new adult renaissance to re-emerge clean and worthy to house the divine spirit.

The mind is renewed then by dislodging false ideas and refilling with a solid soil of thinking based upon our nascent ideals and revealed truths; hence freeing this mind from the long-nested negative bondage. Our Thought Forms have their *image power.* Images are the pictures of the mind's eye. They are concrete and often specific. They accompany our ideas and make them more powerful thus penetrating the subconscious. The old ideas and images that need to be transformed are deeply embedded; fresh and strong ones need to go just as deep to reroute the thoughts through the heart with prayer and re-flection. So we rebuild the mind slowly, idea by idea, passage by passage. *Renewing the mind transforms the emotions* that begin to be expressed as the most powerful force exerted in the physical world. This expression of the mind or heart is the same we put forth while praying or when we convey our love for one another. Effective feelings are the product of positive ideas and images connected to the right behavior.

Emotions are renewed by placing them in subjection to a renewed mind. People of all ages can be enslaved to their feelings of anger, anxiety, malice, rage, lust, and bitterness. The true renaissance does not merely require us to control our negative emotions but to change them altogether. We have to *crucify the sinful nature with its passions and desires.* That is what Jesus did during those forty days of temptation following his water baptism. There and then emotions can become servants and no longer masters. Healthy feelings of joy and humor delight our self-conquest and are essential to the good life. They are made. They don't just happen.

"You have heard that it was said, 'An eye for an eye and a tooth for a tooth.' But I say to you, do not resist the one who is evil. But if anyone slaps you on the right cheek, turn to him the other also. And if anyone would sue you and take your tunic, let him have your cloak as well. And if anyone forces you to go one mile, go with him two miles. Give to the one who begs from you, and do not refuse the one who would borrow from you. (Mat. 5:38.) What Jesus is really promulgating here? Is it the unqualified love and altruism leading to a global Kingdom where a Universal Renaissance prevails? By all means, yes. These directives come very much within the Law of Attraction where the "giver" has the upper hand over the "taker:" If we do not resist the attacker we invalidate, destabilize and weaken his action. We turn the other cheek because we know the force of the blow will wane and in the coming act lays the potential for reconciliation; and as we go the extra mile we extend the person into unbalance and probably remorse, and when we give we extend a helping hand of energy and human benevolence. Here comes the true, superior personality of the spiritually reborn and such are his superior characteristics.

I want to share with you a poem written by Tom Cutts about *"The Man Who Thinks He Can":*

If you think you are beaten, you are beaten.
If you think you are not, you are not.
If you like to win, but you think you cannot,
It is almost certain you won't.
If you think you will lose, you have already lost.
Any success in the world begins with an act of will.
And it is entirely a state of mind.

This is a good material for your meditating or physical exercises. Your subconscious is your built-in homing device; when your mind gives this device an order saying "you failed" then it delivers failure to you. Any man or woman who always thinks about traffic accidents is issuing an invitation to have a traffic accident and will invariably have one. Do you know why? Because the most perfect homing device or computer system is the one God gave man. You ask for an accident and it will be given to you, because "when you ask it shall be given and when you knock it shall be opened."

This is the *Christian Experience* that irrespective of your personal faith or religion you can feel, live through and practice. An experience strengthened by intense feeling and an arising assurance out of the radiant certainty of an indwelling Christian philosophy which presence does not cease to instill wisdom, power and success. Reason can sometimes settle for us what we ought to do but only feeling can make us do it. Positive feelings are the direct results of our achieved spiritual renaissance. Its hidden directives can become firmly established and habitual, leading the currents of the subconscious toward serene and peaceful manifestations.

As the Spiritual Renaissance will happen individually to people capitalizing on these esoteric principles a universal return to spirituality is apparent despite the confusion caused by this age of great scientific and technological wonders. The price of admission is humility. The only casualty will be the loss of egoistic identity. The reward is sanity regained in the form of rationality, innate wisdom and fulfillment. We have all the indications that we will soon move beyond this age of spiritual frivolity to a wiser place where we will have the courage to reject the *milk food* and move forward to spiritual maturity. The hardest part is admitting to the current foolishness. After that just as the past century brought a great scientific explosion, this new century will bring a great spiritual upsurge.

-16-

The Miraculous
Subconscious

"It is done unto you as you believe . . ."

Jesus

J esus' miracles were wrought to set examples for the
human race of what the spirit can do when pursuing
and recognizing his philosophy as a way of life. He even
promised us *greater things we may do*. He did not act to
satisfy people's thirst for sensation or force them to believe
through external events. Hence miracles and cures were always

signs ushering in a larger and more fundamental scheme: the Kingdom of God where *His works are seen;* a realm where decontaminated inner minds hold sway in people who crossed the threshold up to the spiritual renaissance.

This is the reason why the Master shunned his hometown folks' demand for a *sign* and disappointed Thomas' Greek friends who came to see a *miracle,* only to find a man speaking enigmatically about the culture of wheat when he gave them the Sower parable. As to the Pharisees who came and began to put him to the test by asking for a sign from heaven, he sighed deeply and said, *"Why does this generation ask for a miraculous sign? I tell you the truth no sign will be given to it."* Then he left them, went back into the boat and crossed to the other side of the lake. The disciples had only one loaf of bread in the boat. Aware of their concern on the lack of food Jesus asked them: *"Why are you talking about having no bread? Do you still not see or understand? Are your hearts hardened? Do you have eyes but fail to see, and ears but fail to hear? And don't you remember? When I broke the five loaves for the five thousand, how many basketfuls of pieces did you pick up?"* *"Twelve," they replied. "And when I broke the seven loaves for the four thousand, how many basketfuls of pieces did you pick up?" They answered, "Seven." He said to them, "Do you still not understand?"* (Mark 8:11)

Nine thousand people were fed before their eyes at two different locations yet the disciples and the Pharisees wanted a sign! The human sense of reality has a marvelous way of incorporating unusual events. Our minds do not want to see the miraculous and when they encounter miracles they have they unleash their marvelous powers of rationalization to incorporate the miraculous into the humdrum.

Jesus recognized the fact that there are people who need to be able to monitor, count, measure and weigh as in the case of

Thomas who represents *the scientific type* among the disciples. When he got the opportunity to test whether in fact Jesus Christ was standing in front of him after his resurrection Jesus prompted him: *"Be not unbelieving, but faithful"* (John 2:19). He wanted Thomas to apply his new experience by pondering so honestly and deeply so the root of his doubt disappeared and something dawned on him. The fact that Jesus still had to say this afterwards does not mean that Thomas was a skeptic or *forced to believe* even by fear of punishment. It rather means that even after that Thomas kept his ability to personally reach his new conviction. Thomas had to learn that there are other ways of convincing one's self apart from considering the physical facts and Jesus knew what was right for Thomas. He did not want to force anybody. There was no intention to provoke him into refusing something that he was not mature enough to decide on.

When Jesus appeared to the disciples after his Resurrection their first impression was that he was a ghost! So he ate some food to disprove that theory. At one instance he had to persist on them saying: *"See my hands and my feet, that it is I myself; touch me and see, for a spirit does not have flesh and bones as you see that I have."* (Luk. 24:39.) If something doesn't look right we assume first that we're seeing things. Only after we resolve all those possibilities do we take the more dramatic explanation seriously. When NASA put a man on the moon and sent back television pictures to prove it a public opinion poll revealed that most people didn't believe it. They thought it was faked on some sound stage somewhere!

The Pharisees asked for a sign but Jesus sighed and gave them none. Then He castigated the disciples for forgetting about the feeding of the nine thousand for which they bore witnesses. None of them stood up to the Pharisees and said: You want a miracle? Where were you when he fed that multitude? Now you know why Jesus was annoyed. Imagine working miracles for nine thousand people that even your followers forgot, ignored and explained them away. One more miracle won't make any difference at all if we don't pay attention.

Why we should believe a miracle? Because each one of us is a miracle by itself! Let's just consider our origins: we began as a chance meeting between a sperm and an egg swimming around in seminal fluids. They joined together and nine months later we were born. The magnificent structure of our body and the infinite complexities of our human mind is a living miracle that David recognized and praised God for His wondrous work.

The healing powers of the subconscious cured hundreds of the cuts, bruises, sprains and burns since our childhood. Many people were cured from a multitude of diseases that afflicted mankind over the years through their inner powers. I am not taking anything away from God in saying this. God is the healer of all conditions, great or small, but he created this inner healing machine within each of us to serve us in accordance with our faith and belief.

Modern psychiatrists do not accept the reality of demons and exorcism. Demons as asserted in this book are the products of human eccentric negative proclivities. Exorcisms of Jesus are regarded as old-world descriptions of psychiatric problems. Most healings described in the Gospels are now regarded as corrections of psychopathic disorders. The fact that Jesus was merely using his era's language explains the dominating obsession among people that any mentally or bodily ill is stricken by God for his or his folks past sins; hence God's inhabitance in him was replaced by a demon.

Hysterical disorders in a person ensue when his contaminated subconscious tells his conscious brain that they have some kind of obstruction. This wrong programming was altered by Jesus' shock therapy: "*Your sins are forgiven.*" We term it "Shock Therapy" because the Jewish inherited belief was that God alone can forgive sins. Less successfully today hypnosis would enable the subconscious to unleash its remedial instructions and prompt the body to heal, i.e. follow again the right course of nature. Could this reprogramming be a deception? Yes and no. While we cannot deceive the subconscious through our conscious mind, it could be tricked through hypnosis whereby a hypnotized person becomes totally *amenable to suggestion*, meaning he/she would *believe* whatever was told.

In Medical application doctors contend that their medical profession is a very *hopeful* one because *their patients will get better whatever they do*. It is now widely recognized that the placebo effects of the drugs, i.e. the curative effects from simple explanations that drugs will make them whole account for 30% efficacy on any medication. Some doctors treat diseases like dermatitis and hallucinations by simply administering *sterilized water injections*: a message convincingly received by the subconscious mind. The placebo effect is even more important in psychiatry where the power of suggestion is the only applied treatment and the healer's faith in his spiritual power is the criteria; the person's own expectations would pave the road to recovery.

The miracles of Jesus were not the central endeavor of his mission. He only did them in order to help after being asked, not to impress the crowds or broadcast his message. In fact he demanded his disciples and witnesses not to publicize them: "*Go and tell nobody.*" Jesus wanted to give the palpable example to his disciples and followers, as well as to us today of how to revive this dormant energy within us and the latent potential in our mind to generate a surge of divine power capable of healing us and those around us. ". . . *When Jesus* *had come down from the mountain (strong in Spirit), great crowds followed him; and there was a leper who came to him and knelt before him, saying, "Lord, **if you choose** (absolute belief), you can make me clean." He stretched out his hand and touched him, saying, "**I do choose** (positive). Be made clean!" Immediately his leprosy was cleansed. (Mat 8:1.)*

This infinite healing Presence of Life which Jesus called *Father* is the curative catalyst of all diseases whether mental, emotional or physical. It is in the subconscious mind and if faithfully directed can heal the human mind, body . . . and affairs of all illnesses and impediments. This healing power will respond to you regardless of your personal status. It does not care whether you belong to any church or creed as long as Jesus Christ is the basis of your élan. Many "healers" in the Far East and charlatans around the world achieve vast results through the power of mind not through Christ yet the feats performed by Jesus and his disciples are unequalled then and now.

Looking at the healing activities of Jesus we can also study another specific aspect of his teachings. He not only refers as some healers of the present, to the *cosmic energy* that they feel running through themselves. Those modern impostors skim at the surface of what Jesus wanted to convey. He refers to the Father and creator of this cosmic energy and derives his spiritual powers from the very source. The energy is not an abstract force here; but a well traced power generated by the Father enabling man to become His co-creator on this planet. Hence today's spiritual healing and related psychological and spiritual advances cannot be successful outside the dependence on the Father through whom Christ promised we can do even *"greater things than he."*

Shortly after his glorious Ascension two of his disciples Peter and John, who grasped his *way to the Father* did just that using the same technique of the Master: . . . *"Now Peter and John went up together into the temple at the hour of prayer, being the ninth hour. And a certain man lame from his mother's womb was carried, whom they laid daily at the gate of the temple which is called Beautiful, to ask alms of them that entered into the temple; seeing Peter and John about to go into the temple he asked for alms. And Peter, **fastening his eyes upon him with John, said, look on us.** And he gave heed unto them, expecting to receive something of them. Then Peter said, silver and gold have I none; but such as I have I give you: in the name of Jesus Christ of Nazareth rise up and walk. And he took him by the right hand, and lifted him up: and immediately his feet and ankle bones received strength. And he leaping up stood, and walked, and entered with them into the temple, walking, and leaping, and praising God. And all the people saw him walking and praising God: and they knew that it was he which sat for alms at the Beautiful Gate of the temple: and they were filled with wonder and Amazement **(spell)** at that which had happened unto him. (Act. 3:1.)*

Peter fastened his eyes and asked the man: *Look on us* to produce the same trance-like state; the man was in a spell as he *fixed his eyes* upon them and his consciousness was temporarily obstructed. Peter spoke to his subconscious mind and it went into immediate action fixing his withered limbs. When Jesus arose from the dead and they went to the place where his body was, the angel (Jesus himself) appeared to them and they went into a spell. As to those who witnessed the healing of the man brought down from the housetop, they were also put into the subconscious realm or in a spell as they saw the man *getting healed* to keep their conscious minds from creating waves of doubt; the worst of all negative impulses.

Here we saw clearly the element of faith prominent throughout the healing process. Peter healed the born lame (a feat no psychology or charlatanism can achieve today) by his powerful faith in Jesus words: *"Whatever you ask in my name, I will do it."* Besides the element of faith another *process* was required to perform the miracle: alienation of the conscious mind that was achieved by Peter's *fastening his eyes upon him,* whereby he could penetrate and instruct the lame's subconscious mind to heal the body in the name of Jesus. Thus the three basic requirements: obstruction of the sick's conscious, the faith of Peter and the penetration of the lame's subconscious were simultaneously met and the miracle realized.

Blocking the carnal mind that doubts is the hypnosis that allows administration of the subconscious that believes. This is exactly what happened to Paul on his way to Damascus to arraign fleeing Christians to Jerusalem for punishment and here is again the story in his own words: *"And it came to pass, that as I made my journey and was come near Damascus about noon, suddenly there shone from heaven a great light round about me. And I fell onto the ground (from his horse: this severe spell was on a par with a harsh, merciless man to shut off his robust consciousness), and heard a voice (now directly through the subconscious) saying to me: Saul, Saul, why do you persecute me? And I answered: who are you Lord? And he said unto me: I am Jesus of Nazareth, whom you persecute. And they that were with me saw indeed the light and were* **afraid** *(a needed, brief spell to bar any negative interference),* **but they heard not the voice of him that spoke to me"** *(solely directed to Paul's subconscious mind!)* (Act. 22:6.)

Paul was subjected later to further *spells: "And it came to pass, that, when I (Paul) was come again to Jerusalem, even while I prayed in the temple, I was in a spell"* (Act. 22:17.) The Greek meaning for *spell* is to *displace the mind.* It is also translated as *amazement* or *astonishment.* But in any translation it implies the state of the conscious (our carnal mind) put to sleep or hypnosis for the purpose of temporary disablement. As we have already seen accessing the subconscious can best be through stilling the consciousness to perform programming and ultimately rendering it inoperative altogether to achieve miracles.

Historians and naturalists had always a different approach using their all dominant inductive mind. They have never approached the power of the subconscious or measured the positive receptivity of belief. Jesus' miracles were invested with a profound spiritual significance and in each event we can discern beyond the full extent of the *miracle* the great symbolical drive to the dawning Kingdom of Heaven. Historians note without explaining that those who witnessed the miracles *failed to realize* what had really happened. They could be right in this instance as Jesus himself charged them of *not seeing or understanding. With hearts hardened and eyes that fail to see and ears that fail to hear.* Such is the human nature. Historians explain that this reported miraculous act cropped up in the spiritual sphere alone and what really took place was some kind of non-miraculous edifying gesture.

So what in fact did Jesus do? They cannot say for certain. They only rationalize and foist their materialistic interpretations; a process they have been following for hundreds of years. Rationalization drove them to assume that Jesus may have distributed a few loaves to explain a symbolical, universal significance as feeding a multitude provides an excellent sign of universal salvation. Jesus, probably sentient of such expected reactions and to further concretize those feats clearly asked his disciples following the two events: "How many extra basketfuls you lifted?" Obviously the skeptics' reasoning does not traverse the boundaries of their inductive conscious where the element of belief is to them an irrational maze.

Historians and naturalists could speculate endlessly about what ailments Jesus cured and how. They compare such acts to those of many *medicine men* practicing sympathetic magic during the Old Testament era as well as his times. Those surface skimmers would not penetrate deeply into the *obscure zone* where many psychosomatic afflictions have been eased by contact with Jesus' powerful personality. They fail to grasp how very often *a power went out of him and cured them all.* While wondering if Jesus possessed some very special curative gifts they refer to true people who refused to *believe* he had accomplished anything whatsoever. What is really true in this context is the single, paramount criteria: belief.

-17-

The Child Mind of God

"I praise you, Father, Lord of heaven and earth, because you have hidden these things from the wise and learned, and revealed them to little children. Yes, Father, for this was your good pleasure."

Jesus

What the Master is conveying here? Was it the true pleasure of God in hiding this knowledge so simple that little children embody and express, so remote and complex to the wise and learned? Jesus could not put his *birth from water and spirit* message across to Nicodemus and countless *wise* Pharisees but felt it expressed and acted naturally by the little ones. Today we know what he was talking about: If God has hidden something from us let us not think that we will find it out somewhere, like becoming a theologian or a philosopher, it simply means that we have to go back to our childlike mind where God will make Himself known to us.

The following Gospel story depicts Jesus' fervent attachment to children when a crowd of villagers flocked with their little ones for the Master's blessings. They could not get near Jesus! Everyone from town was there. Jesus' disciples stopped them. *"What are you doing here with all of those children?"* asked a disciple. *"We came in hopes that Jesus will bless our children,"* replied a father. *"You must go away now,"* insisted the disciple. *"Jesus does not have time for children. He is very busy talking with important people."* The parents sadly started to leave when suddenly a gentle voice could be heard saying *"DO NOT TURN THE CHILDREN AWAY."* It was the voice of Jesus. *"Bring the children to me."* The crowd moved back to let the children through to Jesus who held out his arms and hugged each one of them. The children made Jesus smile and laugh. *"I wish everyone were like little children, for the Kingdom of God belongs to such as these."*

Much before he washed his disciples' feet, those connected with Christ were likened to *Sheep* (John 10:11.) Christ himself was as well called the *Lamb of God*. The existing openness of the disciples which they had regained from their daily interacting with Jesus is comparable to the Master's relationship with the Father. The disciples had all achieved this *re-born* cycle and although mature they could now feel and act like a blank page or like a child. This process led them to modesty yet innate arrogance had to be overcome time and again. Such insight keeps growing with a significant but intimate relationship with God: humility in a free and spiritual meaning and not some servile behavior but a *sonship relation* Jesus established with the Father that was and still remains often misunderstood.

It is a great tragedy that many non-Christians see the slavery of man before the Almighty as due and appropriate; any alteration to the formula is a clear trespassing by the *created to his Creator*. Jesus associated himself with sinners despite the reproach of the *sage people* of the time just to emphasize his elevating of man to his higher rank out of sinful slavery. Among his most moving words is the parable of the prodigal son which portrays God as a loving father welcoming home the wayward son who squandered his share of the family fortune. *"The slaves,"* says Jesus, *"do not know what the master is doing."* That is the deeper malady. Jesus wanted man to be, as himself, the Father's partner in promoting the Truth and go about it with all the love and exhilaration of that partnership. He meant this partnership to become a fountain of life watering the soil for an ever-greater human harvest that makes man a joint heir of God. It lights his way and lightens his burden enabling him to live in the consciousness that the Father works within him: *"my Father works and I work."*

Jesus humanized God and raised man to a higher pedestal: *"I do not call you servants [or slaves] any longer"* he said to his chosen community. In an era where slavery can have many bad names that was indeed welcome news. The larger problem of slaves is that they are *en-slaved* to a blind obedience. They are not given the whole scope of things. They do not make decisions. They merely follow along in a kind of legal obedience to their master. Jesus reversed this cycle and taught that neither he nor the Father is that kind of master. In that new process where the one that is getting served was not served for the sake of the slaves' own skin a community of love manifested itself: the absolute obedience was transformed into one of a deliberate, joyful association.

This rapprochement also meant that the child-mind of God or the sphere of positivism could be the purer mind of any human. A baby as we had noticed gets a pure subconscious as a birth present soiled only by whatever trivial negativities injected by his mother while in the womb. God has initialized that mind with wholesome thoughts. When growing the child abandons that God-given innocence to learn wickedness through his evolving carnal mind gradually tainting the purity of the innate subconscious. While attaining adulthood his mind looks like a wall filled with evil writing and nasty pictures. Jesus advocated the return to pure mind without dropping its astute aspects: *"Be meek as lambs but shrewd as serpents."* He wanted man to adopt a childlike mind to bring him closer to the functioning of his original subconscious.

Unlike the human mind widely portrayed by psychologists the child-pure mind of God is far different and difficult to attain. Paul says: *"For who has known the **Mind of the Lord**, that he may instruct him? But we have the **Mind of Christ**."* (1Cor. 2:16.) Paul meant that in accessing God's mind the mind of Jesus comes as our role model. God reasons *deductively*! He does not need to gather facts to come to a conclusion. Likewise Jesus' teachings were not reasoning or argumentations but simply final wrappings. He would *start with the conclusions* and *deduce* from there. To say that God reasons inductively (gathering facts in order to reach conclusions) implies that He does not know the conclusions. God always starts with the answer because He already knows every conclusion. He does not need to go on a fact-finding spree to come up with a final answer. Jesus had the same simple, straightforward mind that does not have the *duality* of our mind but rather the childlike promptness and deduction. Jesus was not telling us to become immature babies when he asked us to be like children. He was telling us to *believe* as children do without doubting for a very valid reason that psychologists discovered recently: that is exactly how the subconscious, our inner motivator, operates.

Why we are charmed by our lovely babies and even the cute baby animals? Because the shapes and expressions of their faces invoke something innocent that brings us back to our nostalgic purity. Their radiated rays of purity reflect the face of God, the source of all loveliness! When we evolve to maturity we lose much of this purity because of negative behavior. Fortunately God has the door always open to recreate and reestablish innocence through the cleansing of our inner minds. And in as much as every designer (*repetition*) always expresses in his artwork something of himself, the World Designer expresses His loveliness in those created cute things!

Jesus brings us closer to the point: *"See that you do not look down on one of these little ones, for I tell you that their angels in heaven always see the face of my Father in heaven."* (Mat. 18:10.) If you look down on the childlike mind you look down on the purity and loveliness of God. The mind of a baby is not therefore an empty box; our Heavenly Father has injected in it His pure thoughts and the Master taught us that we have to approach God with the same pure thoughts to reveal His secrets. A child receives *without doubt or mental reservation* any message from his family or contacts; the same messages are accepted likewise and inscribed in his fresh subconscious where the spirit of God dwells.

This is in no way an invitation to be credulous to simple minded people who act childishly in mindless ways that would lead them to conflicts with themselves, but to wisely differentiate between the childlike mind and the childish, erratic behaviors. Paul explains this clearly to the Corinthians:

"Stop thinking like children. In regard to evil be infants, but in your thinking be adults." (1Cor.14:20.) This is a reflection of Jesus' *". . . be shrewd as serpents"* and a reminder that as we grow up negative things grow in us simultaneously that require our vigil watch and better understanding. Adulthood without purity is rebellious. Peaceful and smiling baby faces fade out under the invading negative pressures yielding to gloomy and restless looks: the rebellious spirit changes to proud smugness and dissolute joy.

Any person has the capability when s/he crosses the threshold to understand the subconscious to renew and purify this mind. You can adopt Jesus' related teachings as you are but when you effectively apply them you don't remain as you are. The ensuing renewal in your mind alienates you from conforming to the patterns of your environment. Paul put this notion into words to the Romans: *"Do not conform any longer to the pattern of this world but be transformed by the renewing of your mind."* (Rom.12:2.) A renewed mind is like the anti-virus protection in your computer; it protects against temptations while an unclean mind is an open door to all negativities.

Adult-like mindedness can spell haughtiness, conceitedness and complacency while a childlike mind reflects an unassuming, modest nature that penetrates much deeper than arrogance at the human and spiritual levels. An adult-like question was made by the disciples who came to Jesus and asked: *"Who is the greatest in the kingdom of heaven? He called a little child and had him stand among them. And He said: 'I tell you the truth, unless you change and become like little children, you will never enter the kingdom of heaven.'"* (Mat. 18:2.)

At this time where the Return to Spirituality is evidencing itself gradually perhaps the biggest obstruction facing mankind is the lack of spiritual maturity. People will never find salute and peace of mind until all attitudes of the old creation are put to death and a fresh consciousness of humility and forgiveness opens this mind to the new requisites. A little child cannot talk yet knows how to get his mother's attention. Many adults can talk and discern yet they ignore the way to communicate as Jesus did with the spiritual Father! The world may never change and spirituality may not reach its expected flamboyance until we learn from children . . .

"Of the tree of the knowledge of good and evil you shall not eat, for in the day that you eat of it you shall die"(Gen 2:17.) Thus God commanded Adam according to the biblical illustrative language. Was that part of the great plan He had for man promising him hope and peace of mind? Or was it a *custom made* design befitting our Grandpa's limited mental capabilities as opposed to our era's intelligence? In all probabilities, Adam and his wife wished to be like God thus broke His commandment and destroyed His plan. Their nakedness, God's wrath and the dispossession of their bountiful garden did not deter them from acquiring knowledge. Their shattering of the link that bound them to God caused a mental pain which they tried in vain to suppress. The wisdom we derive from this story is that man's brainpower today is capable to accommodate both earthly knowledge and divine spirituality. The childish story of Adam and Eve entices us to follow Jesus' call for partnership with the Father as His sons and daughters. The road to meet God is clear: children's purity.

"Whoever receives one such child in my name receives me, and whoever receives me, receives not me but Him who sent me." (Mark 9:37.) Jesus encapsulates here the analogy between the three elements of purity in this universe. In this profound truth he not only entices us to consider children as his vivid representatives on earth but also those of God. Loving children means loving him as well as the Father: It is a welcoming and communing step toward God. No wonder Jesus was called the Child Jesus, the Divine Infant, the Baby Jesus, or the Christ

Child. Such names represented Jesus from his birth to the age of twelve.

"But they were silent; for on the way they had discussed with one another who was the greatest." Silent, in expectation of the Master's opinion who *read* their thoughts and they knew they didn't have to ask: *"He sat down and called the twelve; and he said to them, 'If anyone would be first, he must be last of all and servant of all."* Did Jesus presage to destroy the pursuit of greatness? No. He simply addressed the ugly and distorted pursuit and radically transformed it into something beautiful and gratifying. Jesus elevated man to a true significance: the association with his Creator, a dream that obsessed man's imagination since time immemorial. Jesus advocated a new type of greatness: to be truly great without longing to be *known as great as*, or at least greater than someone else . . .

This divine association is equivalent to the integration of the self with the universe and with its highest levels of spiritual reality. The positive values and ideals of the spirit are imperishable. Even that which is true, beautiful, and good will prevail in the human experience. Those realities born of love and nurtured with joy and faith will survive even if man himself does not choose to. And all these things are part of the Universal Creator that Jesus rightfully called Father. The Father is living love; His spirit is in his sons though mortal humans. When all is said and done the *Father image* remains the highest human concept of God.

The Christian credo bore the transcendent fruits of the divine spirit. Jesus' faith was not immature and credulous like that of a child but in many ways it did resemble the unsuspecting trust of the child mind. Yet Jesus interacted with God in as much as the child trusts a parent. He had a profound confidence in the cosmic potential similar to a child's trust in his parental environment. His wholehearted belief in the fundamental goodness of the universe very much resembled the child's dependence on the security of his earthly surroundings. In his reliance on the heavenly Father the correlation seems very much in line with a child leaning upon his earthly parent; he never doubted the care and support of the Father and he obtained it whenever needed. He received this support moment before he resuscitated Lazarus as well as on the eve of his trial. He combined the stalwart and intelligent courage of a full-grown man with the sincere and trusting optimism of a believing child. That in itself is a reflection of How God's child mind performs; certainly on the divine level.

Jesus humanized God and made Him accessible to the cleansed human subconscious. His absolute faith attained the purity of a child's trust. His sense of dependence on the divine was so positive that it yielded the joy and the assurance of absolute personal security. There was no hesitating pretense in his religious experience. Thus the faith of a child always reigning supreme meshed naturally with the giant intellect of the full-grown Messiah in all matters relating to the religious consciousness. Hence his saying, *"Except you become as a little child, you shall not enter the kingdom."* Notwithstanding that Jesus' faith was *childlike*; it was in no sense *childish*.

Perhaps this childlike behavior was best evidenced in Jesus' assault on the Scribes and the Pharisees. He was many times far removed from *the gentle Jesus, meek and mild* who turns the other cheek motivating tolerance and love into a stormy personage with a *mighty vein of granite in his character* giving his opponents as much as he got from them and more. Some of his attacks cannot simply be dismissed as mere Oriental verbiage: *"You are like tombs covered with whitewash; they look well from outside, but inside they are full of dead men's bones and all kinds of filth . . . . You snakes, you vipers' brood, how can you escape being condemned to hell?"* (Mat.23:27.)

This tirade started earlier by the Baptist, may be considered by many a grotesque riposte from the minister of love and compassion. The meek Lamb of God who ordained man to return to childhood to become worthy of the Kingdom of Heaven displays a child's inductive mind, impulsive, spontaneous, non-judgmental and non-restrictive that does not hesitate to call a spade a spade. The mind of Jesus, the same mind of God, cannot flatter, cajole or compromise. And exactly as you cannot fool a child with your feelings towards him; that is how a child does not hesitate to candidly show and express his towards you. The Church and many historians were baffled by the romantic picture of Jesus surrounded by children taking his affection for these innocent beings as a feature of his noble character; obviously they were all unaware of the working of his mind.

Within this child-pure association with Jesus and through him with God we undergo transformation of our likes and dislikes, what we value and disvalue and even define the very entity that we are. Such change in what we will or want makes us recipient of the universal love. When we start experiencing it we see our old sad idols fall away to be replaced by that exhilarating joy and witness a remarkable portrayal of the unselfish love not just manifested or offered but *commanded* by Jesus. We are commanded to love as Jesus loves *in order that* our joy may be complete. We have to receive and treasure his love with thanksgiving in order to love as he loves. This is the way to a devastating joy, the joy of the lord that endures in all circumstances and goes beyond any superficial feeling as described by Nehemiah: "the joy of the Lord is your *strength*" (Neh. 8:10.)

-18-

Afterword

"Take the first step in faith, you don't have to see the whole staircase just take the first step."
Martin Luther King

As you had noticed at several stages, the book you have just read is not a scientific or religious one; it is rather a spiritual and metaphysical approach with guidance to monitor and pursue our spiritual internal dialogue. The various psycho-spiritual theories we have addressed hopefully constitute advanced directions to set the higher goals and ideals and have them materialized. The working of our mind is that when we don't intentionally set our goals then *whatever we think*—or we don't think about our personal aspirations becomes automatically our goal by default. We cannot turn off the brain's goal-seeking mechanism. The subconscious as we have seen works automatically; if we do not volunteer our own objectives that mind is always pursuing some goal whether we are aware of it or not.

In my previous book "Jesus Christ that Unknown" I had addressed with lesser details few of the topics you have gone through. The esoteric psycho-spiritual philosophy of Christ has always been my prime interest ever since I terminated my early academic studies. One thing I did in all those years was read. I read countless books of all sizes on this mammoth subject. I read 50-page and 800-page books and sometimes went twice over some colossal volumes depending on how much I liked and learned from them. However one category of books I read more than any other was on the human mind. In fact I'm sure I read no fewer than 150 books on the subject of the mind alone. Along with that strenuous exercise the repetitive adult reading of the Bible was already nested in my memory since childhood: My grandma wouldn't let me go to sleep every night without reading to her a biblical chapter!

Old Christianity has indeed done a great service to this world but what is now most needed is a fresh comprehension of the real Jesus and his human experience as expressed by those spirit-born mortals who effectively revealed the Master to all men. Rather than reviving primitive Christianity we must go forward from where we find ourselves. Modern culture must become spiritually illuminated with a new revelation of Jesus' life and a fresh understanding of his gospel of eternal salvation. The Master said it bluntly to his early disciples: *"I still have much more to say to you, more than you can now bear. But when he, the Spirit of the truth comes, he will guide you into all truth."* Jesus' modern disciples should become in this era of knowledge an overflowing source of inspiration and enhanced living to all men. Religion is only an exalted humanism until it is made divine by enmeshing the spirit of God with the human experience.

Humanity's spiritual development moves slowly but surely. The slow spiritual development is affected by man's indifference to truly know God, the Universe, and himself. His sightless pride shades him away from the Higher Intelligence and singles him out as the highest product of nature. The 19th century philosophy still sways men to the materialistic sphere. The good news though is that many erudite and scientists are spiritually enlightened beings; culture opened their consciousness to the eternal values. The search for Truth is in progress although many still look for their salvation through mediums outside their entities. Unfortunately the Universe does not function in such a manner. Humans must learn to be responsible and participate in their own spiritual liberation.

The pursuit of Truth requires some discipline otherwise no soul-advancement may be attained. Jesus came to rouse the latent spirits and ushered in intensely the value of time and the purpose of life with all the bliss of the Kingdom of God being the haven of higher human values. As truths always hurt one way or another acquaintance with his message came slow and watchful at first. Yet he knew seeds grow well in the dark grounds of the human subconscious. Many of his precepts were not accepted first; they were vehemently refuted by the same individuals who taught them later as divine principles to others or even to us. This is the marvelous power of Truth and its unstoppable breakthrough.

The various existing religions may consist in traditional beliefs, emotional feelings, philosophic consciousness and punishment for related sins; the teaching of the Master requires the attainment of higher levels of real spirit progression. It is the most dynamic influence ever to activate the human race. Jesus shattered tradition, destroyed dogma, and called mankind to the achievement of its superior ideals on this earth to *"be perfect, even as the Father in heaven is perfect."* It is simply a restoration of the human dignity when all men are declared the children of God. A raised man to the deity's order is automatically reminded through the repeater of his subconscious to follow the same positive highway, heave himself from the negative aspects of human feebleness and chart a lifeline prescribed by the sublime impulses of his educated subconscious.

In real Christianity the virtue of any act must be measured by the motive: the cause of the cause that determines the purpose and the intention that sets out the drive. Jesus was never concerned with morals or ethics of how to act or what to eat; but rather with that inward and spiritual fellowship with the Father which directly manifests itself as the outward and loving service for man. This is the genuine personal experience that man should contain within himself; one that is inevitably displayed in actions and practices that enhance the human brotherhood.

This is the leap from conformity to freedom and from slavery to partnership that entails higher responsibilities, renewed dynamism and vigilant alertness. Perhaps for that reason Jesus almost in all his speeches called people for such watchfulness to become aware and live up to the commands of their rehabilitated consciousness. Commands that are far from the abiding relationship: a free will bind that has the blessing of own's self prior to the heavenly one.

Also by the Author:

- Jesus Christ that Unknown